LEFTIST "LOGIC" IS HURTING *YOU!*

IF LIBERALS BELIEVE strong, independent women can protect themselves, THEN WHY do they oppose the right to own and carry a handgun for self-defense? IF LIBERALS BELIEVE Hillary Rodham Clinton is the ultimate female role model, THEN WHY has she built a political career on her husband's philandering while silencing his many female whistle-blowers? IF LIBERALS BELIEVE Barack Obama is the most pro-woman American president in history, THEN WHY does he seek to make women completely dependent on the federal government? IF LIBERALS BELIEVE the right to an abortion gives women personal autonomy and sexual freedom, THEN WHY are its debilitating aftereffects—from depression to infertility—conveniently overlooked? IF LIBERALS BELIEVE Republicans are so insensitive to women, THEN WHY is the sexual lechery of politicians from Ted Kennedy to Bill Clinton defended, covered up, or ignored?

DISCOVER THE TRUTH ABOUT THE LEFT'S WAR ON WOMEN IN KATIE PAVLICH'S *ASSAULT AND FLATTERY*—AND FIGHT BACK!

"Katie Pavlich blows the lid off the lies the Left tells women . . . and shows them that REAL liberation is thinking—and doing—for themselves. That is TRUE girl power."

—Monica Crowley

Turn the page for more reviews!

"Sharp, factual, and hard-hitting but with a gloss of feminine polish. . . . If you arm yourself with the information found within *Assault and Flattery*, anyone who repeats the Left's tired talking points about the GOP's War on Women is going to find themselves quickly silenced with the facts."

—*Gay Conservative*

"Pavlich is not afraid to skewer the Left's sacred cows, one by one. . . ."

—*Right Voice Media*

"Katie Pavlich stands up for women everywhere by exposing the blatant hypocrisy of the Democratic Party and its phony 'war on women' mantra against Republicans. In fact, as Katie makes abundantly clear, the Democratic establishment has long tolerated misogynistic conduct—from sexism to outright physical abuse—by some of its most notable and beloved leaders. . . . A thorough and gutsy book that should help set history straight."

—Mark R. Levin

"Katie Pavlich shows once again why she's one of the country's top conservative reporters. This fun and engaging book will definitely turn any number of myths about Democrats and their so-called support of women on their head. This is a book to give to anyone in need of being immunized from the false narrative endlessly perpetuated by the mainstream media."

—Sean Hannity

ASSAULT
AND FLATTERY

The Truth About the Left and Their War on Women

KATIE PAVLICH

THRESHOLD EDITIONS

NEW YORK   LONDON   TORONTO   SYDNEY   NEW DELHI

Threshold Editions
A Division of Simon & Schuster, Inc.
1230 Avenue of the Americas
New York, NY 10020

First Threshold Editions paperback edition March 2015

THRESHOLD EDITIONS and colophon are
trademarks of Simon & Schuster, Inc.

For information about special discounts for bulk purchases,
please contact Simon & Schuster Special Sales at
1-866-506-1949 or business@simonandschuster.com.

The Simon & Schuster Speakers Bureau can bring authors to your live event. For
more information or to book an event, contact the Simon & Schuster Speakers
Bureau at 1-866-248-3049 or visit our website at www.simonspeakers.com.

Interior design by Ruth Lee-Mui
Jacket design by Laywan Kwan
Jacket photograph by Claudio Marinesco

Manufactured in the United States of America

10 9 8 7 6 5 4 3 2 1

ISBN 978-1-4767-4960-0
ISBN 978-1-4767-4961-7 (pbk)
ISBN 978-1-4767-4962-4 (ebook)

For Meri Pavlich Roby and Margaret Thatcher

CONTENTS

THE C-WORD

I always cheer up immensely if an attack is particularly wounding because I think, well, if they attack one personally, it means they have not a single political argument left.

—*Margaret Thatcher*

Women of America, you are being lied to. Manipulated. Used. By the mainstream media and the Democratic Party—as if there's a difference—both of which tell you they have your best interests at heart. They don't. The reason I know this is that I've seen firsthand how they treat women who don't toe their line. There's no sign of chivalry or even basic respect for women then.

Many of you have even been persuaded that there is a "war on women" being waged by the other political party. In fact, the real story is very different. The Democratic Party has been at war against women for decades. Those they haven't lied to and brought onto their side have been victimized, demonized, and ridiculed—especially if they dare to speak out with a different point of view.

Don't get me wrong—Democrats and liberals are pretty good at

treating the majority of women like dirt. But they are especially re-
pulsive when it comes to uppity conservative women. To them "conservative" is just as vile a "c-word" as the other four letter "c-word"
they often use to describe us. Their tactics go beyond disagreement
on policy positions and into brutal, misogynistic attacks on women
and their families.

When Rush Limbaugh called thirty-year-old Georgetown law
student Sandra Fluke a "slut" after she testified before Congress and
begged for taxpayers to foot the bill for her birth control, the left had
a field day. Liberals like MSNBC's Krystal Ball organized a boycott
of Limbaugh's sponsors, and he was held accountable for months
even after apologizing.

When liberals use vile language against conservative women,
these same people are hard to find. A deafening silence falls over
politicians, Hollywood celebrities, feminist groups—and the mainstream media that apologize for them all. They get away with a sickening double standard that makes being a conservative woman in the
public eye a punching bag for liberals whose delicate sensibilities go
out the door at the mention of any Republican female officeholder.

Consider the case of MSNBC's Martin Bashir, who in 2013 said
someone should punish Sarah Palin by, in effect, defecating in her
mouth. Bashir's words came after Palin made a comparison between
the national debt and slavery. For the record, Occupy Wall Street
protesters made a similar comparison between debt and slavery. Even
Bashir himself made a slavery comparison in 2011, during another
ad hominem tirade against Representative Michele Bachmann when
she made a pledge to support traditional marriage. He wondered
aloud, "Did Republican hopefuls really sign a pledge suggesting a
return to the days of slavery?"

Outraged at Palin for comparing anything to slavery, Bashir took to his lonely 4:00 p.m. time slot to air his English-accented anger. "And we end this week the way it began, with America's resident dunce Sarah Palin, scraping the barrel of her long-deceased mind and using her all-time favorite analogy in an attempt to sound intelligent about the national debt," Bashir said, playing a clip from Palin's speech. "Given her well-established reputation as a world-class idiot, it's hardly surprising that she should choose to mention slavery in a way that is abominable to anyone who knows anything about its barbaric history."

Bashir then told a story about a brutal slave owner and diarist, Thomas Thistlewood. "In 1756, he records that a slave named Darby 'catched eating kanes had him well flogged and pickled, then made Hector, another slave, s-h-*-t in his mouth,'" Bashir said. "In 1756, this time in relation to a man he refers to as Punch: 'Flogged Punch well, and then washed and rubbed salt pickle, lime juice and bird pepper, made Negro Joe piss in his eyes and mouth.' I could go on but you get the point. When Mrs. Palin invokes slavery, she doesn't just prove her rank ignorance. She confirms if anyone truly qualified for a dose of discipline from Thomas Thistlewood, she would be the outstanding candidate."

Bashir's comments were well-planned, typed into a teleprompter, and approved by an entire production team before being broadcast to his ~~millions of~~ few viewers. But the women of MSNBC, including feminist heroine Rachel Maddow, never uttered a word of criticism. Neither did the National Organization for Women, the Feminist Majority Foundation, or a host of other organizations claiming to fight for the rights of women everywhere.

Of course, the hits against Palin—a popular former governor and three-time *New York Times* bestselling author—didn't start or end with Bashir. As soon as she stepped onto the national stage as

John McCain's vice presidential nominee, nothing about her—or her family—was off-limits to ridicule and personal attacks.

In May 2011, liberal pervert and pornographer Larry Flynt told London's *The Independent*,[1] "Sarah Palin is the dumbest thing. But I made a fortune off of her." Flynt was referring to a porn film called *Nailin' Palin*, based on the Alaska governor. A lifelong exploiter of women, Flynt has made a fortune off of films showing the women he calls "bitches" being gang raped, molested, and murdered in concentration camps.

Flynt's insult and crude film were bad enough, but they were nothing compared to what he said next. "She did a disservice to every woman in America," he said, referring to Palin's newborn baby Trig, who is living with Down syndrome. "She knew from the first month of pregnancy that kid was going to be Down's Syndrome. It's brain dead. A virtual vegetable. She carries it to all these different political events against abortion, she did it just because she didn't want to say she'd had an abortion. How long is it going to live? Another twelve, fifteen years? Doesn't even know it's in this world. So what kind of compassionate conservative is she?"

Naturally, gay activist, former *Daily Beast* writer, and blogger Andrew Sullivan had a similar view on Palin's son Trig. "The medical term for Down Syndrome is Trisomy-21 or Trisomy-g," he wrote. "It is often shortened in medical slang to Tri-g. Is it not perfectly possible that the very name given to this poor child, being reared by Bristol, is another form of mockery of his condition, along with the 'retarded baby' tag?" Blinded by his bigotry, Sullivan failed to note the name Trig comes from the Norse and means "true" and "brave victory." Sullivan later attended a state dinner at the White House at the invitation of President Barack Obama.

Another conservative female politician who receives a load of hate from the left is Minnesota congresswoman and former GOP presidential candidate Michele Bachmann. During her presidential run, the August 2011 cover photo of the now nonexistent and bankrupt *Newsweek* featured an extremely unflattering photo of Bachmann—a normally photogenic woman—looking like a crazy person, with the headline, "The Queen of Rage: Michele Bachmann on God, The Tea Party, and the Evils of Government."

Three months later, Bachmann made an appearance on *Late Night with Jimmy Fallon* to promote her book. Unbeknownst to Bachmann—whose many virtues do not include an extensive knowledge of popular music—the show's band led by a rapper named Questlove played "Lyin' Ass Bitch" when Bachmann was introduced and while she walked across the stage. The song includes the charming lyrics "slut trash can bitch." Neither Fallon nor the band believed anyone would think the prank was inappropriate, because after all, everyone hates Michele Bachmann. Right?

Bachmann is married to Marcus Bachmann, who runs a Christian counseling practice that sometimes counsels gay people. The Bachmanns have five children and helped raise twenty-three foster children, but liberals have decided to take aim at her husband's sexuality. When she announced she would not run for re-election in 2014, the online show *The Young Turks* put together a video with the title, "An Ode to Michele Bachmann & Her Totally Straight Husband," which implied in clip after clip that her husband is gay. Jon Stewart and Jerry Seinfeld "prayed the gay away," on *The Daily Show*, taking a swipe at Bachmann's religious views about gay marriage by insinuating her husband is gay. MSNBC's Lawrence O'Donnell piled onto the gay baiting on his show.

Among the most notable offenders when it comes to slandering conservative women:

DAN SAVAGE: MASTURBATING WHILE PRAYING FOR CANCER

Dan Savage is the founder of the "It Gets Better" campaign, whose mission is to stop the bullying of LGBT youth. Savage doesn't practice the tolerance and kindness he preaches. On May 4, 2013, Savage wished cancer on Sarah Palin: "Woke up to Sarah Palin's voice. She's taken up chewing tobacco now cuz LIBRULS or Bloomberg or something. Now seeing upside of oral cancers."

When Republican Christine O'Donnell was running for the U.S. Senate from Delaware, Savage mocked her religious views about masturbation. Savage declared in a column, "I'm all for masturbating to Christine O'Donnell . . . but why limit it to one day? I hereby declare every day between now and November 2, when O'Donnell's nomination costs the GOP a Senate seat, to be Masturbate to Christine O'Donnell Day. Rub one out for freedom, people!"

ALLAN BRAUER: CRUZADE AGAINST
FEMALE SPEECHWRITERS

LGBT activist Allan Brauer is the communications chair of the Sacramento Democratic Party. On September 20, 2013, he launched into a Twitter tirade[2] against Texas senator Ted Cruz's speechwriter and aide Amanda Carpenter: "May all your children die from debilitating, painful and incurable diseases."

When Carpenter suggested people stop following Brauer, he continued: "Busy blocking the tapeworms that have slithered out of hellspawn @amandacarpenter's asshole. How's your day so far?" he wrote. "I'm being attacked on Twitter for wishing one of Ted Cruz's pubic lice to experience pain her boss is inflicting on Americans."

In response, the California Democratic Party backhandedly issued an apology, blaming the incident on Ted Cruz.

"The problem with this kind of rhetoric is that it lets fringe characters—those who are actively trying to shut down the government—like Ted Cruz, off the hook," spokesman Tenoch Flores said in a statement to *Yahoo News*. "It's never acceptable to wish physical harm against political opponents, regardless of how objectionable their policy priorities are."

This wasn't the first time Brauer had an outburst. His archive of tweets is very colorful, especially toward conservatives.[3] "Your mamma called," one reads. "She wants her Obama dildo back, but please wash your sh*t off it first." Another, directed at a conservative female activist, says, "It's cute how you butt in where you're not wanted, like herpes."

PROGRESS KENTUCKY

Republican Senator Mitch McConnell has been in the United States Senate since 1985 and doesn't have any intention of leaving in 2014, but Progress Kentucky, a radical liberal group in the Bluegrass State, wants him gone badly enough that they were willing to help fund a Tea Party candidate to oppose him. Their other campaign tactic? Making racist comments[4] about his wife, former labor secretary Elaine Chao. The Harvard-educated conservative was the first Asian-American to hold the position.

Chao was born in Taiwan in 1953, after her father fled China to escape communism. When she was eight years old, she moved to the United States. Before her work in the government, Chao excelled in the private sector through work at Bank of America, Citicorp, and The United Way.

Despite her impressive resume, Progress Kentucky, a group that *surely* embraces diversity, tweeted, "Is #MitchMcConnell too close to China? Dissident Wu 'very surprised' at Chao pick."

They continued, "Mitch and his $$$ have VERY strong ties to #China (that place your job moved to)." They added, "This woman has the ear of @mcconnellpress—she's his #wife. May explain why your job moved to #china!"

When confronted with the statements, Progress Kentucky spokesman Curtis Morrison refused to retract them or issue an apology, and the group's executive director, Shawn Reilly, refused to acknowledge any racial undertones or wrongdoing.

DAVID LETTERMAN: IN PRAISE OF STATUTORY RAPE

In June of 2009, sixty-two-year-old Late Night creep and serial adulterer David Letterman thought it would be hilarious to make a sex joke about Sarah Palin's daughter. "One awkward moment for Sarah Palin at the Yankee game, during the seventh inning, her daughter was knocked up by Alex Rodriguez," Letterman joked. Palin went to that Yankee game with her daughter Willow, who was fourteen years old at the time.

The Alaska governor and her husband, Todd, were less than impressed. "Acceptance of inappropriate sexual comments about an underage girl, who could be anyone's daughter, contributes to the atrociously high rate of sexual exploitation of minors by older men who use and abuse others," Sarah Palin said in response.

"Any 'jokes' about raping my fourteen-year-old are despicable. Alaskans know it, and I believe the rest of the world knows it, too," Todd Palin added.

Letterman eventually apologized (kind of), but he later made clear that he apologized only so that he could continue to make fun of her on television. "I felt like Sarah Palin was somebody I wanted to be able to continue to make fun of," Letterman said on *Oprah's Next Chapter*. "And I felt like if I don't apologize, I will not be able to go forward [with the jokes]."

BILL MAHER: DROPPING THE C-WORD ANY TIME HE CAN (WHEN REFERRING TO A REPUBLICAN)

Shortly after Republican Texas senator Ted Cruz finished his twenty-two-hour-long filibuster in protest against Obamacare, HBO host Bill Maher took the opportunity to opine on what women active in the Tea Party movement think about during sex with their husbands. "Its official," he tweeted, "women in the Tea Party have replaced Rand Paul with #TedCruz as the guy they think of when their husband is humping them."

Two years earlier, while critiquing a debate performance by Texas governor and GOP presidential candidate Rick Perry, Maher opined, "Sarah Palin was watching and she said, 'If only he was black, I'd f*ck him.'"

Maher's history of outrageously sexist statements includes calling Palin a "MILF" (which stands for "mother I'd like to f*ck") and "dumb c*nt," because "there's just no other word for her"[5]—which was so outrageous that even NOW came to Palin's defense. He's also taken perverted swipes at her daughter Bristol, suggesting in 2012 she name her new book *Whoops, There's a D*ck in Me*, and said, "Bristol Palin has to admit that the reason she f*cked Levi over and over until a baby fell out is because she liked it. . . . Bristol, just admit it. You were horny." (Maher has also attacked Congresswoman Michele Bachmann as a "dumb twat.")

After Maher's misogynist "jokes," there was pressure on Barack Obama's Priorities USA Action Super PAC to give back the $1 million Maher had donated. But Bill Burton, the head of the group and later Obama's senior spokesman, refused. He excused the comments as "comedy" and distinguished them from Rush Limbaugh's insult of Sandra Fluke (which prompted a massive loss of advertising dollars, a phone call from President Obama to Fluke, and an apology from Limbaugh). Burton said, "The notion that there is an equivalence between what a comedian has said over the course of his career and what the de facto leader of the Republican Party said to sexually degrade a woman who led in a political debate of our time, is crazy."

GUY CIMBALO: A REPUBLICAN RAPE LIST

In January of 2009, *Playboy*'s Guy Cimbalo shared the top ten Republican women he'd like to "hate f*ck," or in other words, rape, in an article titled, "So Wrong, It's Right."[6]

"There is a way to reach across the aisle without letting principles fall by the wayside. We speak, naturally, of the hate f*ck. We may despise everything else these women represent, but god*mmit they're hot. Let the healing begin," Cimbalo wrote.

Got that? According to Cimbalo, the implication of rape is a valid solution to disagreeing with a woman's politics.

Here's the list of women he put together, along with the horrific descriptions. The women were also given a "hate f*ck rating":

#1 MICHELLE MALKIN: "This highly f*ckable Filipina is a massively popular blogger who is known to dress up like a cheerleader on occasion (see video). She's also a regular on Fox News, where her tight body and get-off-my-lawn stare just scream, 'Do me!'"

#2 MEGYN KELLY: "You need to flagellate your genitals for wanting to f*ck this woman."

#3 MARY KATHARINE HAM: "You get this one pregnant, she stays pregnant. Karma's a bitch, isn't it?"

#4 AMANDA CARPENTER: "She's got the look of a 1940s vixen with whom we'd like to do some very 2009 hate f*cking."

#5 ELISABETH HASSELBECK: "Endlessly perky, this golden goddess probably has her Catholic school uniform still in the closet and she wouldn't mind putting it on before taking it off for a session of sweaty, anti-American hate f*cking."

#6 DANA PERINO: "The second she says 'no comment,' your testicles are going to retract back into your body."

#7 LAURA INGRAHAM: "Vaginal dentate would be an improvement."

#8 PAMELA GELLER: "A stone-cold ZILF (i.e. Zionist I'd Like to F*ck) in possession of a thick Long Island accent and a top-heavy frame."

#9 MICHELE BACHMANN: "She's rumored to have a Clinton-level libido and with that batshit-crazy look in her eyes you know she's a screamer."

#10 PEGGY NOONAN: "Despite her obvious poise, we can't escape the sense that she'd be up for some meaningless, Cheever-esque hate f*cking after a few gin and tonics."

After outrage from women on both sides of the aisle, *Playboy*, which has touted itself as a women's rights organization, refused to apologize, although it did at least pull the piece. Instead, it sent a statement to Fox News saying, "*Playboy* has a long and proud history of supporting women's organizations, and has been an advocate of equal rights for women since its inception more than 55 years ago. The feature on Playboy.com was by no means intended to insinuate or encourage violence against women—something the organization adamantly abhors. It has been removed from the site."

Cimbalo is now a contributor at the liberal *Huffington Post*.

LARRY FLYNT: PHOTOSHOP PORNOGRAPHY

The most anti-woman liberal in America might be Larry Flynt. We've already seen how this longtime foe of Republicans and friend of Democrats—James Carville even played a lawyer in Hollywood's homage to the pornographer, *The People vs. Larry Flynt*—attacked Sarah Palin and her son Trig. In May of 2012, his magazine *Hustler* created and published a sexually explicit picture of conservative columnist and TV personality S. E. Cupp looking as though she was performing oral sex, asking, "What would S. E. Cupp look like with a dick in her mouth?" Its caption read "No such picture of S. E. Cupp actually exists. This composite fantasy is altered from the original for our imagination, does not depict reality, and is not to be taken seriously for any purpose."

MSNBC'S MISOGYNISTIC SEXIST NABOBS BLOVIATING ON CABLE: ED SCHULTZ, KEITH OLBERMANN, LAWRENCE O'DONNELL

We've already covered Martin Bashir's inanities, so it should come as no surprise when I say that MSNBC is a Mecca for sexist liberals. Ed Schultz is among the biggest of the MSNBCs—Misogynistic

Sexist Nabobs Bloviating on Cable. In 2011 he called conservative radio show host Laura Ingraham a "right-wing slut" and a "talk slut"—whatever that means. Ingraham later pointed out that the leading liberal lady of *The View*, Barbara Walters, "kind of laughed it off. She was like, 'Joy, you call me that word all the time.' And they kind of just laughed. But when [Sandra] Fluke goes on *The View* yesterday, it was 'Oh, isn't this a tragedy' and 'Oh, isn't this horrible' and 'Rush Limbaugh should be driven off the air.'"[7]

Before he was fired in 2010 by MSNBC, anchor Keith Olbermann said that without "the total mindless, morally bankrupt, knee-jerk, fascistic hatred," conservative columnist Michelle Malkin "would just be a big mashed-up bag of meat with lipstick on it."[8] Once he made his way over to Al Gore's Current TV, Olbermann tweeted about conservative columnist S. E. Cupp: "On so many levels she's a perfect demonstration of the necessity of the work Planned Parenthood does." Olbermann claimed he wasn't insinuating Cupp should have been killed inside the womb, until he later apologized.

Cupp got the last laugh when Olbermann got fired from Current TV, when she said, "I am very sorry your TV career has just been aborted."

Chris Matthews, another MSNBC perennial who, in all fairness, is an equal-opportunity misogynist, makes women the frequent butt of insults and jokes on *Hardball*. Matthews has called Hillary Clinton "she-devil," "Nurse Ratched," "Madame Defarge," "witchy," "anti-male," and "uppity." Matthews, however, has reserved the worst for the Republicans he lampoons daily. He has pondered the all-important question of whether Sarah Palin is even "capable of thinking." After calling Michele Bachmann a "balloon head," he said she was "lucky we still don't have literacy tests out there."

MSNBC has at its motto "lean forward." Maybe it's meant as

encouragement to all of its hosts to be as offensive as they can be. The network long ago gave up any pretense of delivering straight news to its viewers. It apparently also gave up any pretense of being a defender of women's rights. If half of the filth uttered by MSNBC hosts ever came out of the mouths of Fox News hosts, liberal women's groups would be leading a charge for an advertising boycott of the network. Picket lines would form outside Fox studios.

When it comes to demonizing conservative women, American Democrats are not alone. Liberals in other parts of the world can be just as sexist, hostile, and offensive, as British liberals showed in April 2013, when the nation's first female prime minister passed away at the age of eighty-seven.

Margaret Thatcher was a pioneer for women, an icon of conservatism, and a titan in British history. Through her partnership with other Cold Warriors like Ronald Reagan and Pope John Paul II, she helped millions of people escape the oppression of communist totalitarianism.

When news of her passing hit the wires, liberals in the UK began to riot in celebration. Liberals took to the streets drinking champagne, shooting off fireworks, and holding signs that read, "Rejoice, Thatcher is Dead," and, "Socialist worker! Rejoice! Rejoice!" They climbed to the top of the Ritzy cinema in Brixton in order to change the theater sign to "Margaret Thatchers Dead, LOL," and to hang a banner that read, "The bitch is dead." They threw "death parties" and began looting local businesses. A building in London was spray painted with the words, "Rot in hell, Maggie Thatcher." The *Mail Online*[9] reported, "In ugly scenes mirrored in cities across the country, dozens of officers put on riot gear and used shields and batons when the crowd refused their requests to disperse. The mob pelted them with missiles, damaged a police car and set wheelie bins alight at the party in inner-city Easton."

Margaret Thatcher deserved better. But she shouldn't have expected better. She saw firsthand the hypocrisy of liberals who claim to support women's rights but who can't stand strong women, unless those women agree with everything they say.

Margaret Thatcher not only knew those type of liberals. She defeated them.

And one day soon, I believe American women will beat them, too.

Pay close attention to what I've just told you: These are leaders of the left who have held back no invective against women they don't control. They've revealed their real feelings and their real contempt toward the female gender. To the left, we are just reckless, helpless, sex-crazed messes who need Big Daddy to come in, rescue us, and keep us safe from ourselves. And I can prove it. So let's get started.

Part I

INSIDE THE REAL WAR AGAINST WOMEN

CHAPTER 1

VAGINA VOTERS

That's right, I voted with my lady parts.
—*Democratic voter in Virginia*

The commonwealth of Virginia was one of our nation's first colonies, the birthplace of American presidents, and the beloved centerpiece for the struggle for independence. It is now being run by a hack crony of Bill and Hillary Clinton's. As of January 2014, professional sleazebag Terrence M. McAuliffe became the governor of the historic commonwealth, sitting in the chair once occupied by Patrick Henry and Thomas Jefferson.

For those of you blessed enough not to know who he is, his list of political crimes is notorious. He was the chief money grabber for the Bill Clinton campaign, with no campaign law or regulation he seemed unwilling to skirt. He was the fundraiser who wrestled an eight-foot-long alligator in exchange for a campaign contribution. He was the political addict who complained about not being able to raise money in the days after September 11.

"I was one of our party's most visible spokesmen and I had to keep a low profile after the attacks," he whined in his book *What a Party*. "I was like a caged rat. I couldn't travel. I couldn't make political calls. I couldn't make money calls. I couldn't do anything. I went to my office and worked with my staff to prepare for when we could finally come back out again that made me feel a little better, but basically there was nothing for us to do in the immediate aftermath."

He was the investor who made over $8 million on a company called Global Crossing, which later filed for bankruptcy and handed out ten thousand pink slips. He was also the crazy-eyed campaign manager for Hillary Clinton in 2008, so devoted to and delusional about the Clintons that he was proclaiming her "the next president of the United States" after Obama clinched the Democratic nomination.

Of the classic bad boys the good women seem to fall for, McAuliffe is Exhibit A, a slick-talking guy who always tells you what you want to hear and then does whatever he pleases. This prince of a fellow left his wife in the delivery room at the hospital so he could go out and raise money for his left-wing buddies. "I was trying hard not to appear restless," he writes in his book, "but I am not one to sit still for long and soon I was going stir-crazy, which drove Dorothy nuts." He didn't behave any better with his second child. As the *Washington Post* reported, "McAuliffe left his wife and newborn son in the car with an aide while he schmoozed for 15 minutes at [a] party." That's a fact—that he's proud of this ought to make anybody nauseated.

What's even more sickening is that Governor McAuliffe, with the crucial support of the media, managed to turn himself into the candidate of women while pillorying his Republican opponent for months as being a modern-day Marquis de Sade.

Virginia's well-known and once popular attorney general Ken Cuccinelli became the most recent Republican to find himself drowning under vicious attacks by the Democratic Party machinery for his alleged hatred of women. Silly Cuccinelli—he wanted to talk to voters about improving the state economy, bringing jobs to Virginia, and easing the burden on small business. All of this was drowned out in commercial after commercial aired by McAuliffe that portrayed the state's attorney general as a heartless Neanderthal who wanted to drag Virginia women into a cave and force them to have babies. McAuliffe's $30 million campaign included the carpet bombing of spurious ads linking Cuccinelli to opposition to no-fault divorce and abortion, and it drove the Republican's numbers among women into the ground. The ad about divorce stated, "If Cuccinelli had it his way, a mom trying to get out of a bad marriage, over her husband's objections, could only get divorced if she could prove adultery or physical abuse or her spouse had abandoned her or was sentenced to jail." This was bunk: Cuccinelli's position was completely gender neutral. Similarly, the ad about abortion stated that Cuccinelli "wants to make all abortion illegal . . . even to protect a woman's health"; however, Cuccinelli believed abortion should be legal when the mother's life was in danger.

For months, Attorney General Cuccinelli was accused of being a women's rights extremist. The McAuliffe campaign sent flyer after flyer to homes in Democratic-heavy Northern Virginia warning of Cuccinelli's plan to ban birth control should he become governor. Ironically, just before Election Day, the accused rapist Bill Clinton and his female abuse enabler Hillary Clinton made their way to Virginia for a "Women for McAuliffe" event. I'm sure Bill Clinton was especially excited to go there—he probably picked up a whole list of phone numbers.

In the end, McAuliffe carried the single women vote by 42 percent, six points more than Obama had the previous year, and the overall women's vote by eight points. Since the Democrat won by less than three percentage points, the women's vote made all the difference.

Why Democratic politicians seem so proud of ending the lives of children is a problem for their psychiatrists. But how McAuliffe—the man who applauded, extolled, apologized for, and made millions parlaying his service for serial sexual assaulter and Misogynist-in-Chief Bill Clinton into a job greasing the palms of fundraisers and green energy magnates—was able to get away with turning his *opponent* into a woman hater is a problem for Republicans. How on earth did Republicans allow a Clinton acolyte whom the liberal outlet *Slate* described as "beginning his reign of sleaze" when he was elected and who wasn't even from the state manage to follow in the steps of Patrick Henry and Thomas Jefferson?

Even after McAuliffe won the election, MSNBC's Ed Schultz, the liberal commentator who once called Laura Ingraham a "slut" on the air, hosted a panel, otherwise composed completely of women, to discuss just how extreme Ken Cuccinelli was on women's health issues. In a six-minute panel discussion, the terms "radical," "extreme," "extremist," and "extremism" were used nearly a dozen times.

Schultz's opening question went to alleged comedy writer and founder of Lady Parts Justice Liz Winstead. Such a hilarious and brilliant political commentator was she that her analysis included gems like, "The extremist Republican Party has become so extreme." Then there was this:

> SCHULTZ: A takeaway we can have from last night, it's probably
> not really good to go radical on women. Liz, how do you
> read the results from last night based on who and what
> Cuccinelli was all about?

WINSTEAD: Well, I think that women like sex and I think that
when you run a guy who doesn't seem to enjoy sex, he's not
going to win with women. Am I wrong?

SCHULTZ: Well, I have no arguments with sex.

The above exchange deserves a few comments. For one, thank you Liz Winstead for making women look as if they vote based on how much they like sex through immature and childish arguments. Second, if a Republican had said, "I have no arguments with sex," to a panel full of women, he'd be berated as a sexist pig. Third and for the record, Ken Cuccinelli has seven kids and we all know how babies are made.

Meanwhile, over at the online magazine *Slate*,[1] legal correspondent and left-wing columnist Dahlia Lithwick proudly announced her approval of a friend's Facebook post that read, "That's right. I voted. With my lady parts," and "Cuccinelli: bad for vaginas, oops bad for Virginia." She elaborated, "You can dismiss all the Virginians—men and women—who posted on Facebook today about their lady parts, and their aversion to forced ultrasounds, and the weird feeling they get when the state regulates consensual sodomy as silly sheep who were led astray by an expensive McAuliffe smear campaign. But most of them knew a year ago, sometimes much earlier than that, what Gov. Cuccinelli would mean for their freedom to do what they wanted, with whom they wanted, without government's oversight."

Cuccinelli's campaign never "went extreme" on women, it was the McAuliffe campaign that brought social issues into the picture. This was something Cuccinelli failed to adequately respond to and hoped would go away. It didn't. McAuliffe painted Cuccinelli as an extremist who wanted to control consenting adults, gay and straight, inside their bedrooms.

"Republican Ken Cuccinelli lost to Democrat Terry McAuliffe in Virginia's gubernatorial race Tuesday, thanks in part to Democratic opponents who successfully portrayed Cuccinelli as a medieval anti-women, anti-gay, conservative extremist," a *Huffington Post* article stated shortly after the election.

The left and the media threw a fit over Cuccinelli's support of anti-sodomy laws, laws he strongly defended by arguing they're necessary to properly prosecute child sexual predators. The hoopla started when Cuccinelli challenged a decision by a three-judge panel on the U.S. Court of Appeals for the Fourth Circuit to strike down Virginia's anti-sodomy law based on a March 2013 Supreme Court ruling in *Lawrence v. Texas*. That decision struck down a ban on oral and anal sex between consenting adults, "adults" being the key word. Cuccinelli challenged the panel decision and asked for a full fifteen-judge court to reconsider in relation to a case that involved a seventeen-year-old girl and forty-seven-year-old sexual predator William Scott McDonald. McDonald was convicted of soliciting sexual acts from a minor. Federal Judge Albert Diaz, an Obama appointee who sat on the panel, sided with Cuccinelli on the case. Virginia prosecutors have been using anti-sodomy laws for decades to throw creeps in prison where they belong. Cuccinelli wanted to continue using these laws to put child predators away, including McDonald.

"This case is not about sexual orientation, but using current law to protect a 17 year-old girl from a 47 year-old sexual predator," Cuccinelli spokeswoman Caroline Gibson said in a statement to the *Washington Post*. "We agree with the dissenting opinion that the petitioner was not entitled to federal habeas corpus relief and the full court should have the opportunity to decide this matter. The attorney general is committed to protecting Virginia's children from predators who attempt to exploit them and rob them of their childhood."

Somehow, women's rights advocates took this position as offensive and a threat to women's health. As a member "in good standing" of the National Organization for Women, I take particular offense to what this organization is doing in my name.[2]

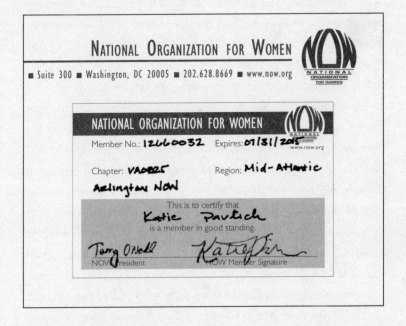

On the night of McAuliffe's victory, for example, NOW sent out an email praising a "progressive path forward for women."

"Today was a victory for women in Virginia. By electing NOW-endorsed candidates Terry McAuliffe and Ralph Northam to the top offices in the state, voters ensured that Virginia can now be on a progressive path forward for women. Women will have better access to health care—including abortion and birth control," the email said.

Ken Cuccinelli never took the time to address birth control bans directly and he lost 67 percent of single female voters because of it. You'd think Cuccinelli, being an attorney, would make it clear to birth control ban conspiracy theorists that the Supreme Court precedent, ahem, *Griswold v. Connecticut*, makes it illegal for state legislatures to ban contraception.

Terry McAuliffe was the candidate out of step with women's views on abortion. He favors late-term taxpayer-funded abortions and loose restrictions on abortion clinics that leave women even more vulnerable to abuse or death (see Kermit Gosnell, coming up). Quinnipiac polling regularly shows 60 percent of women favor a ban on late-term abortions after five months of pregnancy.

Meanwhile, two hundred miles north in New Jersey, Governor Chris Christie was re-elected in a landslide with a female Democratic opponent. Even with a record of stripping Planned Parenthood funding in the Garden State and a pro-life position on abortion, Christie was able to rake in 57 percent of female votes and avoided the paint-by-numbers "war on women" attack throughout his campaign. How? Democrats knew the war on women tactic against Christie would have fallen flat on its face and the candid governor would have immediately called the "war" what it is: ridiculous. This type of rhetoric doesn't work on those who choose to push back with full force against it, as Christie did on *Meet the Press*: "I'm pro-life. I believe in exceptions for rape, incest, and the life of the mother. That's my position, take it or leave it." It was that kind of authenticity that appealed to women and men alike.

Unfortunately most Republicans don't know how to fight back. The mainstream media have been playing this game for a few election cycles now, while Republicans look like chumps. The way they've done it is to create phony controversies that garner far more media attention than is ever deserved. Some examples:

"WOMEN'S HEALTH"

For a long time, liberals have been winning elections on the broad issue of women's health, which for Democratic candidates comes down to abortion and birth control. Liberals paint women's issues with the broad women's health brush in order to avoid talking about the issue of abortion and what abortion really is.

When it comes to true women's health, it's conservatives, not liberals, who want women to know all of their options. This is why legislation has been passed requiring doctors and nurses inside abortion clinics to inform women about all the details regarding their pregnancy before performing a procedure. So-called women's groups like Planned Parenthood regularly oppose lawful requirements that give women as much information as possible about their health and well-being.

In campaign after campaign, Democrats have touted Obamacare as a success for women and as a government program that would bring women quality affordable care without letting the government get in between a woman and her doctor. At the end of the 2012 election, with Obama back in office, in the name of "women's health" Obamacare did the complete opposite of what Democrats promised for women. Premiums for women doubled, coverage was dropped completely for millions, and the doctors women liked and wanted to keep were no longer available. The flashy model of political campaign tactics came home to roost.

WENDY DAVIS

In the summer of 2013, the Texas State Legislature prepared to pass legislation banning abortions after five months of pregnancy, when most fetuses are considered viable, and to require abortion clinics to meet the health and safety standards of a surgical facility (health and safety standards are good things, right?). The law was proposed after Dr. Kermit Gosnell, according to a grand jury, "regularly and illegally delivered live, viable babies in the third trimester of pregnancy—and then murdered these newborns by severing their spinal cords with scissors." In his Philadelphia clinic Gosnell regularly "overdosed his patients with dangerous drugs, spread venereal disease among them with infected instruments, perforated their wombs and bowels—and, on at least two occasions, caused their deaths."

Pro-abortion Texas state senator Wendy Davis made a last-minute decision to stand against the legislation. She grabbed her now famous pink running shoes and started a filibuster at 11:10 a.m. that would end eleven hours later in a liberal "victory." In matching burnt orange T-shirts, pro-abortion activists gathered outside the Capitol Rotunda in downtown Austin to cheer her on. Tens of thousands tuned in on a live stream to watch and #standwithwendy was trending worldwide. At the 8:40 p.m. mark, President Obama tweeted his support by saying, "Something special is happening in Austin tonight." That tweet got 17,243 retweets and 6,594 favorites. The HBO star Lena Dunham also tweeted support to millions of followers. Pro-abortion activists on the Internet went nuts with pro-Wendy memes. Media outlets glorified her for weeks, and MSNBC went so far as to stamp their logo on Wendy Davis quotes about women and their bodies. In the September issue of *Vogue*, a glamorous Davis photographed in the Texas Capitol Rotunda was plastered across the glossy pages with a glowing and lengthy profile attached.

When the same, renamed legislation Davis opposed passed with overwhelming support three weeks later, that didn't stop the fund-raising machine. Democratic groups all over the country ranging from EMILY's List to the DNC jumped on the Wendy Davis bandwagon to raise money for their election war chests. Davis alone raised $933,000 in just two weeks from more than fifteen thousand donors. The majority of the money came from inside Texas, but nearly a third of it was funneled in from out of state. In just over a month, Davis raised more than a million dollars. Davis was an abortion extremist sensation and a money machine, too.

In August, Davis was invited to the National Press Club, where she refused to express support for any type of restriction on abortion. When asked about the details of the Kermit Gosnell trial, Davis played dumb and pretended to know nothing about the horrifying case. Two months later, she announced her candidacy for Texas governor against Attorney General Greg Abbott.

Davis portrayed herself as a struggling, divorced and single teenaged mother who lived in a trailer park. Davis claimed she made her way through Texas Christian University with scholarships and student loans and eventually independently made her way through Harvard Law School. Overcoming struggle was the theme. She said in a campaign video that her story is a Texas story voters can relate to. They say everything is bigger in Texas, and Davis's mistruths about her personal story, a story she's used to woo voters and donors, are no exception.

The *Dallas Morning News* exclusively reported about Davis's story of struggle on January 20, 2014:

Davis was 21, not 19, when she was divorced. She lived only a few months in the family mobile home while separated from her husband before moving into an apartment with her daughter.

A single mother working two jobs, she met Jeff Davis, a lawyer 13 years older than her, married him and had a second daughter. He paid for her last two years at Texas Christian University and her time at Harvard Law School, and kept their two daughters while she was in Boston. When they divorced in 2005, he was granted parental custody, and the girls stayed with him. Wendy Davis was directed to pay child support.

Divorce papers show Jeff Davis cited adultery as a reason for divorce, which allegedly took place during her time at Harvard. In the same interview, Jeff Davis revealed Wendy Davis left him almost immediately after he paid off her Harvard loans. He paid for the rest of her time at law school with money from his cashed-in 401(k).

"It was ironic," he said to the paper. "I made the last payment, and it was the next day she left."

Davis excused the misrepresentation of her life by saying, "My language should be tighter." After being called out on her dramatized and false story, Davis doubled down.

"My story of struggle and sacrifice is not unique—it is the story of millions of Texas women. Our opponents are scared of that truth," Davis spouted off on Twitter. "The other side has reached a new low—attacking my family, my education and playing politics with something that is deeply personal."

The left's new feminist hero turned out to be a fraud.

"BEING A WOMAN IS NO LONGER A PRE-EXISTING CONDITION"

On the campaign trail, women have been told in race after race that, before Obamacare, they were being discriminated against because of their gender. In 2013, the Democratic Senatorial Campaign Committee said Republican Senate candidates who oppose Obamacare are "waging an assault on critical health care services for women," adding that if "Republicans had their way . . . being a woman would be considered a preexisting condition." Likewise, Democratic senator Barbara Mikulski said, "We will not go back to the dark ages where being a woman was considered a preexisting condition."

Patronizing, to say the least, but let's look at the facts. Women are far more complicated than men. They do have children, after all. They're the Cadillac of the human body. Statistically, women visit the doctor more and consume more health care. Therefore, their health-care costs are greater.

Contrary to popular belief, big bad insurance companies aren't simply charging women more money because they can. We don't have a sexist health insurance industry. Health-care companies are simply charging women more for health care because they cost more and require more care.

To start, women typically live longer than men, requiring and consuming more care long-term. Second, women are built differently than men and sustain injuries more easily. Based on doctors' visits alone, women tend to take part in more preventive medical services than men do. They're also less stubborn when it comes to treating injuries or illness with medication and are more likely to take prescription drugs, which are paid for through insurance.

Frankly, I don't regret the fact that, compared to the average man, the average woman lives longer, thinks farther ahead, and is less stubborn. I just don't think actuaries are sexist for knowing this.

A 2012 National Women's Law Center report[3] shows women between the ages of fifteen and forty-four spend 68 percent more on health care than men in the same age range because they're using more services. Similarly, an exhaustive 2000 study from the National Institutes of Health concluded, "Women have higher medical care service utilization and higher associated charges than men. Although the appropriateness of these differences was not determined, these findings have implications for health care." The same study showed, "Women had a significantly higher mean number of visits to their primary care clinic and diagnostic services than men. Mean charges for primary care, specialty care, emergency treatment, diagnostic services, and annual total charges were all significantly higher for women than men; however, there were no differences for mean hospitalizations or hospital charges. After controlling for health status, sociodemographics, and clinic assignment, women still had higher medical charges for all categories of charges except hospitalizations."

EQUAL PAY FOR WOMEN

Continuing the theme of victimhood, Democratic campaigns often capitalize on the argument that women get paid less than men for the same work and that Republicans are okay with that. We've all seen the headlines: "Women earn 76 cents for every dollar men make"—a statistic based on a 2011 report produced by the White House just in time for an election year. But the report, at best, is misleading. Despite Democrats repeatedly hitting the campaign trail with a platform of equal pay for women, the United States has had equal pay laws on the books since 1963 when the Equal Pay Act was passed. In 1964, Title VII of the Civil Rights Act banned gender-based wage discrimination. Both of these pieces of legislation were further bolstered in 1972 with the Equal Employment Opportunity Act.

Salaries for men and women come down to one basic thing: choices. Men tend to go into high-paying careers. Women generally choose professions that pay less. We see the same trend with college majors: Men typically choose degrees with greater financial reward in the workplace than women do. Women overwhelmingly pursue majors in social work, studio arts, communications, human services, and teaching while men make up more lucrative majors like engineering and business. Each industry pays differently based on the job, not based on gender.[4] Women typically take time out of our working lifespan to do things like care for children and adjust work priorities based on family needs. Men work more hours and consecutive years during a lifespan and therefore earn more money.

Although Democrats looking to get elected aren't willing to acknowledge these basic economic facts, surprisingly, NOW board of directors member Warren Farrell is willing to recognize them and wrote an entire book titled *Why Men Earn More*.

"Jobs that expose you to the sleet and the heat pay more than those that are indoors and neat," Warren argues.

A 2009 study[5] conducted by CONSAD Research Corporation for the U.S. Department of Labor further showed the gender wage gap is a nonfactor. "This study leads to the unambiguous conclusion that the differences in the compensation of men and women are the result of a multitude of factors and that the raw wage gap should not be used as the basis to justify corrective action. Indeed, there may be nothing to correct. The differences in raw wages may be almost entirely the result of the individual choices being made by both male and female workers," the study states. More data from the Department of Labor shows men work 8.14 hours per day on average compared to women, who work 7.75 hours, and considerably more women than men work part-time jobs, which tend to pay less.

Women are overwhelmingly doing better economically than their male counterparts. According to the Census Bureau, more women are going to college than men, women are on pace to be making more than men by choosing more lucrative college majors, and more women are employed than men straight out of college, a far cry from being held down through employers' paying less based on gender. The gender pay gap is another example of keeping women in a victimhood mentality to score votes and isn't based in economic fact. The Independent Women's Forum has described the gender wage gap as "feminist fiction."

For years, Democrats on Capitol Hill have been pushing for another layer of employer bureaucracy through the Paycheck Fairness Act, which is based on false numbers and the debunked gender pay gap. The Paycheck Fairness Act would have also provided a treasure trove of new work for trial attorneys by encouraging more lawsuits that include more employees. Under the law, a class action lawsuit would scoop up all employees in a company unless a specific employee went through the effort of opting out. The proposed law also fails to take into account reasons why people in a company, including women, get paid differently based on work experience, time in the field, number of years at a company, and so on. In April 2013, Nancy Pelosi took advantage of failing equal pay legislation to attack Republicans.

"The GOP blocked the Paycheck Fairness Act in the 110th, 111th, and 112th Congresses. Today is the day to get on board with equal pay," Pelosi said at the time. Her colleague in the Senate,

Patty Murray, spun the Paycheck Fairness Act as a potential raise for every working woman in American to close the "pay gap." In a proclamation, President Obama wrote the following: "To grow our middle class and spur progress in the years ahead, we need to address longstanding inequity that keeps women from earning a living equal to their efforts. That is why I have made pay equity a top priority—from signing the Lilly Ledbetter Fair Pay Act days after I took office to cracking down on equal pay law violations wherever they occur. And to back our belief in equality with the weight of law, I continue to call on the Congress to pass the Paycheck Fairness Act."

Like Pelosi and Murray, Obama ignored the fact that his administration pays women 13 percent less than men. Instead, he made a meaningless declaration that April 9, 2013, is "National Equal Pay Day." Mark your calendars, ladies!

Eventually, the Paycheck Fairness Act failed in the Senate because the numbers just didn't add up, but liberals were sure to tell women they were victims beforehand.

Without question, the left saw its greatest success using such tactics in 2012—when an unpopular president facing a troubled economy and a disastrous health-care law pulled out all the stops to terrify women into re-electing him anyway.

When Election Day finally rolled around, Mitt Romney lost women voters 55–44 percent, and the *Huffington Post* credited Obama's victory to the gender gap. Women's groups celebrated.

Terry O'Neill, president of the National Organization for Women, spared no cliché in gloating about their triumph: "In a truly pivotal election, women voters rejected the Romney-Ryan war on women and chose moving forward over taking a giant step backward," she said. "Women demonstrated that civil rights are for everyone, including same-sex couples, and that reproductive rights are hardly a diversion from the dominant issues of jobs and the deficit—they are a central issue in our lives, part of our basic health care and an essential aspect of our economic well-being.... As we celebrate our victories in these elections, we call for an immediate and unconditional end to the war on women that has been waged by right-wing extremists for too long now. We call on Congress and the White House to take action immediately to achieve real equality for women. Women's access to the full range of reproductive health services—including abortion and birth control—must not be subject to politicians' whims or ideologies. We urge enactment and full enforcement of policies to close the gender wage gap."

Cecile Richards, president of Planned Parenthood, also exulted in how the Democrats' strategy succeeded. "This election sends a powerful and unmistakable message to members of Congress and state legislatures all around the country that the American people do not want politicians to meddle in our personal medical decisions," she said in a statement. Unless of course it's for a massive takeover of our health-care decisions. (Planned Parenthood supported Obamacare.)

What these lieutenants of liberalism neglected to claim credit for was their year-long effort to systematically mislead American women and scare them with phony issues and hyperbole. How this success unfolded for the left is worth examining because, of course, they're planning to do it all over again.

In 2012, it was clear even in January that former Massachusetts governor Mitt Romney was likely to win the Republican Party's nomination. Romney had many admirable qualities, ones that might appeal to moderate and independent voters. For one, he had a reputation as a consensus-building manager who'd governed one of the most liberal states in the nation. He had been married for forty-four years to a woman who'd survived breast cancer and is living with MS. Together they raised five children, who by all accounts are devoted to their parents. For the Democrats, this was a problem.

That month, George Stephanopoulos moderated a Republican primary debate in Goffstown, New Hampshire. From the outset, Stephanopoulos, who came to national attention as a Democratic activist and apologist for Bill Clinton, was an odd choice for the debate. He claimed to be a nonpartisan "serious journalist" for ABC News. But it was also well-known that he was desperate to score points with the Clintons, who'd disowned him years ago for a tell-all book he wrote after leaving the White House. So "serious journalist" Stephanopoulos decided to soften up the most likely GOP candidate—Romney—for the general election. The tactic he used laid the groundwork for attacks on nearly every GOP candidate running for office in the future. There is, in fact, no other realistic explanation for what happened that night.

After asking a series of relevant questions about foreign policy and the economy of all the candidates, Stephanopoulos abruptly and awkwardly turned his attention to Mitt Romney and the question of banning contraception, a topic completely out of left(wing) field.

STEPHANOPOULOS: Governor Romney, do you believe that states
    have the right to ban contraception? Or is that trumped by a
    constitutional right to privacy?

MITT ROMNEY: George, this is an unusual topic that you're
    raising. States have a right to ban contraception? I can't
    imagine a state banning contraception. I can't imagine the
    circumstances where a state would want to do so, and if I
    were governor of a state—

STEPHANOPOULOS: Well, the Supreme Court had ruled on that . . .

ROMNEY:—or a legislator of a state, I would totally and completely oppose any effort to ban contraception. So you're asking, given the fact that there's no state that wants to do so, and I don't know of any candidate that wants to do so. You're asking: Could it constitutionally be done? We can ask our constitutionalist here. [AUDIENCE LAUGHS AS ROMNEY TURNS TO RON PAUL]

STEPHANOPOULOS: I'm sure Congressman Paul . . . [INAUDIBLE] . . . but I'm asking you: Do states have that right or not?

ROMNEY: George, I don't know whether the states have a right to ban contraception. No state wants to. I mean, the idea of you putting forward things that states might want to do that no state wants to do and asking me whether they could do it or not, is kind of a silly thing I think. [AUDIENCE APPLAUSE]

STEPHANOPOULOS: Hold on a second. Governor, you went to Harvard Law School. You know very well this is based on—

ROMNEY: Has the Supreme Court, has the Supreme Court decided that the states do not have the right to provide contraception?

STEPHANOPOULOS: Yes, they have, in 1965, *Griswold v. Connecticut*.

ROMNEY: I believe in the, that the law of the land is as spoken by the Supreme Court, and that if we disagree with the Supreme Court—and occasionally I do—then we have a process under the Constitution to change that decision, and it's known as the amendment process, and where we have—for instance, right now, we're having issues that relate to same-sex marriage. My view is we should have a federal amendment to the Constitution defining marriage as a relationship between a man and a woman. But I know of no reason to talk about contraceptions. . . .

STEPHANOPOULOS: Would you accept the Supreme Court decision finding a right to privacy in the Constitution?

ROMNEY: I don't believe they decided that correctly. In my view, *Roe v. Wade* was improperly decided. It was based upon that same principle. And, in my view, if we had justices like Roberts and Alito, Thomas and Scalia, and more justices like that, they might well decide to return this issue to states as opposed to saying it's in the federal Constitution. And, by the way, if the people say it should be in the federal Constitution, then instead of having unelected judges stuff it in there when it's not there, we should allow the people to express their own views through amendment and add it to the Constitution. But this idea that justices—

STEPHANOPOULOS: Should that be done in this case?

ROMNEY: Pardon?

STEPHANOPOULOS: Should that be done in this case?

ROMNEY: Should this be done in this case to allow states to ban contraception? No. States don't want to ban contraception, so why would we try to put it in the Constitution? With regards to gay marriage, I've told you that's when I would amend the Constitution. Contraception, it's working just fine. Just leave it alone.

Though he gave good answers to this odd line of questioning, Romney looked confused. Nothing in the Republican primary, at the state level or in the news at the time, had anything to do with a ban on contraception, but Stephanopoulos asked about it anyway. And he was relentless—with what seemed a blatant effort to target and shake up the GOP frontrunner, and likely nominee.

Stephanopoulos dragged on the discussion with Romney for more than three and a half minutes and inspired a number of boos from the audience before Ron Paul and Rick Santorum were then allowed to weigh in. Many commentators watching the exchange, from all sides of the political spectrum, found it troubling. One pundit compared Stephanopoulos to Tommy Lee Jones from *The Fugitive*. The respected political commentator Michael Barone called the contraception effort pure "partisan game playing" and said, "There really is no reason for Stephanopoulos to have brought this forward than to hurt the Republican candidates."

But there was a reason. The former Clinton operative Stephanopoulos was signaling the Democrats' new line of attack. No doubt because he had discussed it that morning with his best friends—Democratic attack dogs Paul Begala, James Carville, and Rahm Emanuel. As the nonpartisan D.C.-based website Politico noted in 2009, Stephanopoulos is in regular daily phone contact with these three old pals—all fiercely partisan Democratic operatives allied with the Clinton and Obama campaigns.

"I refer to it as the 17-year-long conference call," said Emanuel, who starts calling his friends at 6:00 a.m. "You can tap into it anytime you want."[6]

Since Stephanopoulos is a Democrat and he's helping the Democrats, most of the mainstream media totally ignored this blatant conflict of interest. They've also turned a blind eye to the facts that the Clintons have never forgiven Stephanopoulos for writing a tell-all book about them when he left the White House and that he's been trying to impress them and get back in their good graces ever since. Of course, if Roger Ailes had been conspiring over the telephone with Mitt Romney or Speaker John Boehner—EVERY DAY FOR SEVENTEEN YEARS—Rachel Maddow and Chris Matthews and the other left-wing loudmouths in the media wouldn't stop screaming about it.

Meanwhile, in 2012, Stephanopoulos helped his pals out again in a big way. He was in fact the hatchet man who started the meme that a pro-choice (at least at one time) grandfatherly guy from Boston was going to be climbing in women's windows at night and snatching their birth control from them. Stephanopoulos specifically targeted Romney on the issue because he knew Romney would win the Republican nomination. Considering the economy was in the toilet, he knew Democrats needed to bring social issues back into the picture in order to win. The goal was clear: Make Mitt Romney, the future GOP nominee, look as if he's for banning birth control, which will then trickle down into other races. I'm sure his pals on his phone calls were gleeful.

A few weeks after that debate, on January 20, 2012, the question of contraception burst onto the national scene as a major issue when the Obama administration announced that faith-based schools, hospitals, and nonprofits would be required to provide insurance coverage to their employees for contraception. The White House later attempted to modify the mandate amid outcries from religious groups and conservatives that the mandate was an attack on religious freedom, but the compromise didn't mollify many of the plan's critics.

Shortly thereafter, the Democrats created one of their periodic media sensations. This one came from a pathetic spotlight grabber with political ambitions named Sandra Fluke, a thirty-year-old adult child and Georgetown Law student who was invited to testify before a congressional panel by Nancy Pelosi. She testified that young women needed their neighbors and other hard-working taxpayers to pay for their birth control. Her argument that government should condone and subsidize promiscuity led Rush Limbaugh to infamously label Fluke "a slut," giving liberals and the Obama campaign an opportunity to present Fluke as an even bigger victim of GOP hate.

The Democratic National Convention that summer in Charlotte became ground zero in the war on women. On the same night birth control heroine Sandra Fluke spoke, warning of a grave future under a Republican president that would send women back to an "offensive, obsolete relic of our past," serial sexual assaulter and accused rapist Bill Clinton spoke. Then a lengthy tribute to Ted Kennedy, who left a woman to drown and mistreated countless mistresses since, played with the words "women's rights champion" plastered across the big screens. Along with deadbeat dad Jesse Jackson was Chuck Schumer, who famously called an airline stewardess a "bitch" after she had the nerve to ask him to turn off his cell phone. Notably absent from the proceedings was one of the party's leading presidential candidates, John Edwards, who was still dealing with issues that came with denying the existence of a child he fathered out of wedlock while his wife was dying of cancer.

None of these guys were abandoned by leftist women's groups, of course. Their fury was somehow targeted at Mitt Romney, perhaps the most milquetoast, nonthreatening candidate nominated for president since Warren G. Harding promised a "return to normalcy."

During the second debate of the 2012 election cycle, a town hall format was used, opening up questions to the audience. Katherine Fenton, a twenty-four-year-old preschool teacher from Long Island, asked Barack Obama and Mitt Romney directly about the issue of women's rights in the workplace and equal pay.

"In what new ways do you intend to rectify the inequalities in the workplace, specifically regarding females making only 72 percent of what their male counterparts earn?" she asked.

Obama ducked the question by talking about the Lilly Ledbetter Act—which merely changed the time limits for filing some workplace discrimination suits—and by touting Pell grants and government handouts for women across the country. He also understood he was being asked a question by a young, single woman and quickly diverted to the easily manipulated, politically caustic issue of birth control.

"Governor Romney feels comfortable having politicians in Washington decide the health-care choices that women are making. I think that's a mistake. In my health-care bill, I said insurance companies need to provide contraceptive coverage to everybody who is insured, because this is not just a—a health issue; it's an economic issue for women. It makes a difference. This is money out of that family's pocket," Obama said in response.

Obama then went on the offensive. "Governor Romney not only opposed it; he suggested that, in fact, employers should be able to make the decision as to whether or not a woman gets contraception through her insurance coverage. That's not the kind of advocacy that women need. When Governor Romney says that we should eliminate funding for Planned Parenthood, there are millions of women all across the country who rely on Planned Parenthood for not just contraceptive care."

Naturally, as he did with most of his answers, Romney began to reference his experience during his time as governor. What followed was one of the more memorable Romney-isms from the campaign trail.

> Important topic and one which I learned a great deal about, particularly as I was serving as governor of my state, because I had the chance to pull together a Cabinet and all the applicants seemed to be men. And I went to my staff, and I said, how come all the people for these jobs are all men?
>
> They said, well, these are the people that have the qualifications. And I said, well, gosh, can't we, can't we find some women that are also qualified?
>
> And, so we took a concerted effort to go out and find women who had backgrounds that could be qualified to become members of our cabinet. I went to a number of women's groups and said can you help us find folks? And I brought us whole binders full of, of women.

The answer went on for another minute, where he talked about his management style, in which women with children were allowed and encouraged to take flexible schedules. He also was honest about the wreckage of women's jobs created by Obama's economy: Women lost 580,000 jobs in Obama's first term. Compared to four years earlier, three and a half million more women were in poverty.

But nobody cared about facts like that, especially the media. Not when they had a new gaffe to cover that helped advance their narrative. Romney's line about "binders full of women" immediately went viral. Women's groups, the DNC, and the Obama campaign seized on the opportunity to paint Romney as a clueless candidate whose only familiarity with qualified women came from referring to a folder handed to him by some aides.

In an interview for this book in 2013, I asked Governor Romney what he had meant to say. His answer was a lot more articulate than was characterized in the media at the time—unfortunately it came two years too late.

"As you probably know," he told me, "the University of New York at Albany did a survey of all fifty states to see which governors had placed women in senior positions and found in my administration half of our senior positions were filled by women and that by the way made us the number one state in the nation in terms of women participating in senior management in an administration.

"I think standing back I could tell you that it was very much our effort in both the Olympic experience that I had as well as in state government to have a senior management team which was as broadly representative of the nation as possible. What I found was that if one only relies on word of mouth and recommendations from friends you tend to get the same people, which they often exclude women and minorities. So what we did in state government and in our effort to expand participation of women, was to approach the groups like the League of Women Voters and other groups that had interest and awareness of highly effective women and asking them for help in identifying people who might be able to fill senior positions. They provided us with book, binders if you will, of women's resumes and then we invited these people to be interviewed and I found a number who I felt were ideally suited for the positions we were looking for."

Unfortunately, in that same interview, he indicated how big a problem Republicans have in dealing with the "war on women."

For starters, Romney said something that I hope is untrue. "You know, I didn't pay much attention to the flurry of activity on the left [about his women's rights record]." He needed to pay attention to that and so did his team. If you don't understand how your record is being mischaracterized by your enemies, then how can you possibly rebut the accusations?

This comment was followed by something else that Romney thought was true. "I think virtually everybody who was aware of the debates, and that was a lot of people, understood that I was describing an effort to get resumes of a large number of women and that about one half of the senior leaders of my team were women." Actually they didn't understand that at all, which is why he had a problem he needed to solve. Romney seemed to give women voters more credit than they deserve when he added, "Well, there are a lot of outrageous lies I just don't think women believe so I'm not sure how damaging they are."

Governor Romney said something else that was quite troubling and hard to follow. "I think as you look at the exit polling from the 2012 presidential race you'll see that the place where I and my campaign fell down the most was with minority women and we have to make a much better effort taking our message to Hispanic women, African-American women and other minorities," he said, correctly. "Among the majority population, the white population, I believe among all women, I was able to garner the majority," Romney added, a statement that seemed to make him proud, defensive, and confused, all at the same time. Romney lost among "all women" by eleven points. The former governor might have been referring to white women, whom, according to exit polls, he won by 14 percent, but that's not close to fixing the gender gap. He lost black women by 93 percent, Hispanic women by 53 percent, and other nonwhite women by 35 percent. Romney seemed to think that all Republicans need to do is target their message to more minority women— whatever that is supposed to mean—and they'll be fine. What he is missing is that this is a trend that is getting worse, not better. Even

Romney's margin of victory among white women was thirteen points worse than his margin among white men. Those numbers are only going to get worse.

This of course isn't all Romney's fault. He had the unenviable task of leading a party with Republican men so clueless on "women's issues" they sounded like total idiots, especially damaging in an election year. When Missouri Republican Senate candidate Todd Akin was asked by a local television interviewer whether abortion should be legal in the case of rape, Akin said, "It seems to be, first of all, from what I understand from doctors, it's really rare. If it's a legitimate rape, the female body has ways to try to shut the whole thing down." Richard Mourdock, a Senate candidate in Indiana, said, "I think even when life begins in that horrible situation of rape, that it is something that God intended to happen."

In the future, Republicans must train candidates, especially men, to come up with better answers to avoid playing defense on a single issue for the remaining time of a race.

The 2014 election cycle is bound to be just as exciting as the historic 2010 elections, which means Democrats will be clinging to their war on women and demagoguery to squeak out victories. The Democratic National Committee made their 2014 campaign strategy crystal clear when they hired former EMILY's List executive director Amy Dacey as the executive director of the Democratic National Committee.

"Amy brings a wealth of knowledge, experience, and strategic insight that will be instrumental in helping the DNC continue to grow [and] build on the electoral gains we made in 2012," DNC chairwoman Debbie Wasserman Schultz said at the time of Dacey's hiring.

The playbook is simple: Abortion. War on women. Birth control.

Repeat. Republicans better be ready to counter it, which they acknowledged in post-presidential-election analysis.

"In 2012, the Republican response to this attack was muddled, and too often the attack went undefended altogether. We need to actively combat this, better prepare our surrogates, and not stand idly by while the Democrats pigeonhole us using false attacks," an RNC report said.

Looking further down the road to 2016, with Terry McAuliffe handing Hillary Clinton the swing state of Virginia through the female vote, Republicans better find a way to combat the war-on-women strategy in other swing states before it's too late.

How many elections will they lose before coming up with some kind of coherent messaging against it? Here's a start: We don't want to ban your birth control, ladies. End of story. Period.

The GOP might also actually take a moment to mine an impressive history on women's issues that almost everyone seems to have ignored. Including, sadly, the GOP.

CHAPTER 2

LYNCHING THE GOP

Barring the chilled, scandalized feeling that always overcomes me when I see and hear women speak in public, I derived a good deal of whimsical delight . . . from the proceedings.

—*Democratic Party hero Woodrow Wilson*

I declare to you that woman must not depend upon the protection of man, but must be taught to protect herself.

—*Susan B. Anthony, Republican*

This is a book about the Democratic Party, not the GOP. But no one can explain how toxic Democratic politicians are for women without explaining how much they lie about Republicans and their history. In that history, there is much for Republicans to be proud of, even if they don't know it. For every Todd Akin, there's a Jeannette Rankin. It was the Republican Party that made possible the passage of the constitutional amendment guaranteeing women the right to vote, as well as the anti-discrimination laws of the 1960s protecting women and minorities. Only after these laws were passed did Democrats swoop in to manipulate and hijack the voters that the GOP brought into the political system. It is worth taking a moment to remember this history when it comes to civil rights in general.

In 1870, a black pastor named Hiram Revels made his way to Washington, D.C., from Mississippi. Revels had served in the Civil War as a chaplain for two black Union regiments that he had helped recruit and organize. He saw combat against the Confederacy at Vicksburg. Though he was born a free man to free black parents of African and European descent, railroad conductors and steamboat captains still required him to sit in segregated colored compartments. All of this despite the fact that he had been elected to the U.S. Senate by the Mississippi state legislature as a Republican. Yes, a Republican. Upon arriving in Washington, Revels hoped that he would be the first African-American to serve in Congress, the first African-American to take full advantage of the rights naturally owed to him by serving his country and the people of Mississippi. The only thing standing in his way was the Democratic Party.

As soon as his credentials were read, southern Democratic senators objected to his nomination, arguing that, as of 1870, Revels had only been an American citizen for two years. The Fourteenth Amendment giving former slaves the full rights of citizenship—which Democrats had opposed in any way they could—had only been passed in 1868, meaning that in their interpretation, Revels had only been a citizen for two years. He had to have been a citizen for at least nine years to take a seat in the Senate.

Undeterred, Revels went on to serve the GOP and his country honorably. In his first address to the Senate, Revels defended his own party, arguing, "The Republican Party is not inflamed, as some would . . . have the country believe, against the white population of the South. Its borders are wide enough for all truly loyal men to find within them some peace and repose from the din and discord of angry faction."

Now, on its face, an African-American's journey to the U.S. Senate more than 150 years ago may seem to have nothing whatsoever in common with today's war on women. And yet it has everything to do with it. It is representative of the same whitewashing and routine distortion of their history that Democrats employ to wipe away the discrimination that was at the heart of the party for decades and nearly a century.

Hiram Revels's story is representative of the political reality of the first seventy years of the growing civil rights movement, led by the Grand Old Party. The most famous of abolitionists—Frederick Douglass, Harriet Tubman, Booker T. Washington, and Sojourner Truth—were all Republicans. Republicans passed the Thirteenth, Fourteenth, and Fifteenth amendments, along with the 1866 Civil Rights Act. The first twenty-one African-Americans to serve in Congress were members of the Republican Party. While this makes sense considering the Democratic Party's chronic opposition to civil rights efforts, a more practical barrier was the embarrassing reality that blacks were not even permitted to attend Democratic conventions in any official capacity until 1924.

The truth is that the civil rights movement was hijacked by the left the moment that their political interests coincided with advancing civil rights and only at that moment. President Franklin Delano Roosevelt saw an opening in splintering the Republican lock on the black vote when he calculated that millions of African-Americans hit especially hard by the Great Depression would buy into the big-government promises of the New Deal. Regardless, FDR—the darling of the liberal project and utopia—was no civil rights advocate. Racial discrimination was often a part of New Deal programs, whether directly or indirectly. FDR refused to betray the southern Democratic wing of his party and oppose anti-lynching legislation and poll tax laws.

Even as the demographic shift with African-Americans support-ing Democrats continued, the Republican Party never abandoned its advocacy of the civil rights movement. In the twenty-six major civil rights votes after 1933, the Republican majority favored civil rights in over 96 percent of the votes. By contrast, a majority of Democrats opposed civil rights legislation in over 80 percent of the votes. Presi-dent Eisenhower and Senate Republicans were the drivers behind the landmark but expediently forgotten Civil Rights Act of 1957, which created an important Civil Rights Commission and Civil Rights Division in the Department of Justice. The left's reading of history forgets that Eisenhower had two other critical parts in his bill to promote civil rights—both of which were fought and politically defeated by Democrats. It was Senator Lyndon B. Johnson who led the campaign to defeat Eisenhower's stronger push for school deseg-regation and a reform of civil suits to remove racial bias.

As for LBJ, he is extolled in history as a liberal icon, the man who signed the most important civil rights legislation into law. But his motivations were far from pure. He once boasted, "I'll have those n****rs voting Democratic for the next two hundred years."[1] (LBJ was also no slouch when it came to manipulating women—usually into uncomfortable positions right in front of his wife, Lady Bird.)

Thanks to the collective amnesia of the mainstream media and the shameful fact that history doesn't seem to be taught in public schools anymore, the Republicans' essential contributions to passage of the landmark Civil Rights Act of 1964 have been all but erased. Eighty percent of Republicans voted for the bill, while less than

70 percent of Democrats did. Among those Republicans voting for equality were Donald Rumsfeld, Bob Dole, and Gerald Ford.

Even today the media love to remind us that Republicans like Barry Goldwater opposed the 1964 Civil Rights Act. Never mind that Goldwater and Republican opponents to civil rights were a minority among the party or that their opposition did not stem from racial prejudice but from well-intentioned concerns of con-stitutionality. And let's conveniently forget that there were many more prominent Democrats who opposed the bill, too—such as Al Gore, Sr., William Fulbright, and Robert Byrd, a KKK member who personally filibustered the law for fourteen hours. Byrd was later called a "mentor" by Joe Biden, and Nancy Pelosi said he "strove to build a brighter future for us all." (By "us all," she apparently didn't mean black people.) When Byrd died, Bill Clinton all but defended his KKK membership at the funeral by saying he was just "a coun-try boy" trying to get elected. By the way, which party—in 1977 and again in 1987—elected that former member of the Ku Klux Klan as the leader of the United States Senate, third in line to the presidency? The Democratic Party of Dianne Feinstein and Barbara Boxer and Al Franken. And just as they have rewritten the narrative of their own party and its racist members, they have falsified the his-tory of women's rights by erasing the trailblazing role of Republicans from the nation's collective memory.

THE PARTY OF JEANNETTE RANKIN

The hijacking of the civil rights movement reveals the liberal mind-set. It is not one of inclusion, but one that betrays naked po-litical calculation, and the same discriminatory undertone that they accuse the GOP of having. It's all about extortion and using specific carved-out groups to gain politically, not to actually help as Democrats often claim. Understanding this mind-set makes it crystal clear which party is actually waging a war to subvert "women's rights" for political gain. It's the party that consistently voted against securing fundamental and equal rights for American women. Yes, you're right again. It's the Democratic Party.

In November 1916, after campaigning across the entire length of the Big Sky state, women's rights activist and feminist Jeannette Rankin achieved a milestone in American history. She became the first woman elected to the Congress of the United States of America. And she was elected as a Republican. Rankin's goal was to take the fight for women's rights to Congress as a voice for the concerns of millions of suffragettes in the halls of Congress. Her opponents? The Democratic representatives, senators, and President Woodrow Wilson—better known to the suffragettes as "Kaiser Wilson," an allusion to the German monarch.

The battle Rankin sought to bring to Washington from Montana had been decades in the making. It had been fought by Republican activists like her who had been thwarted at every turn by a Democratic Party intent on keeping women out of national politics. The Democrats were afraid that women's rights would be a sort of gateway drug to lull the nation into support for black rights. As Georgia's state senator (and Democrat) J. J. Flynt explained, female suffrage "works in fundamental opposition to the fundamental principles of our party" because it "was mothered by Susan B. Anthony and her kind of northern woman who were close associates of Thad Stevens and Stephen Douglas and who sought to put the black heel on the white neck and place the southern Negro in power." (Flynt likely meant Frederick Douglass, the abolitionist and friend of Anthony, not Stephen Douglas, the racist who ran twice against Abraham Lincoln.)

In 1872, the Republican Party was the first to approve a resolution in its platform favoring the admission of women to "wider fields of usefulness" and added delicately that "the honest demand of this class of citizens for additional rights . . . should be treated with respectful consideration." In 1878, California Republican A. A. Sargent introduced the Nineteenth Amendment, known as the Susan B. Anthony Amendment, for the first time. The Democratic Senate voted it down, sparking the Republican legislative battle for suffrage. The GOP introduced the Nineteenth Amendment to Congress every year from then on, only to have it bottled up in various committees and strangled in procedural red tape for another decade before either chamber was allowed to vote on it. In 1887, it finally reached the floor of the Senate. It was defeated again by a Democratic Senate by a vote of thirty-four to sixteen, the second of four times that a Democratic Senate would vote down the Susan B. Anthony Amendment to grant women the right to vote.

But the GOP and its suffragette allies wouldn't give up that easily. They pursued other avenues. Working at the state level, a variety of Republican-controlled states, including Wyoming, Colorado, and Idaho, granted women suffrage for state and local elections. Rallying the suffrage movement and the Republican Party together, Rankin achieved her greatest goal just two years after arriving in Congress: universal women's suffrage. Despite over forty years of Democratic opposition, Rankin and the GOP secured equal political rights for women. The new majority Republican House's first action was to call for a vote on an amendment to the U.S. Constitution.

Representative James R. Mann, a Republican from Illinois, reintroduced the Nineteenth Amendment in the House, and it passed by an overwhelming majority. The now Republican-controlled Senate was the next key to breaking the Democratic block on women's suffrage. Standing true to their principles, the final tally was thirty-six Republicans for, eight against, and twenty Democrats for, seventeen against. The amendment was then sent to the states. The trend was resoundingly the same. Twenty-six of the thirty-six states that ratified the Nineteenth Amendment had Republican legislatures. Of the nine states that voted against ratification, eight were Democratic—including J. J. Flynt's Georgia.

So began the historic role Republicans have played in the women's rights movement. The same party that sent Hiram Revels to serve his fellow countrymen as the first African-American in Congress sent the first woman, Jeannette Rankin. The same party that battled blatant racists at the local, state, and federal level battled sexists. The same party that sought to end lynching and the poll tax sought to end women's pay discrimination and grant women the right to vote. Yes, the Republican Party.

HIJACKED

The Democrats opposed the GOP's fight for women's rights—until, of course, it was politically expedient for their larger agenda. What better example of the liberals' "miraculous" swing toward supporting the rights of women than the presidency of Woodrow Wilson, the "progressive" himself? The man who gave us the income tax, the Federal Reserve, and a naïve liberal foreign policy still looked to today. Not coincidentally, Wilson was also a man who was "deeply racist in his thoughts and politics, and apparently he was comfortable with being so." In office, he segregated employees at all federal offices and created a culture of politically legitimized discrimination. Woodrow

Wilson, whom the Left cheers for being so "progressive," led the first wave of hijacking women's rights in textbook fashion.

"Barring the chilled, scandalized feeling that always overcomes me when I see and hear women speak in public, I derived a good deal of whimsical delight...from the proceedings." This is how a young Woodrow Wilson described a meeting of the Association for the Advancement of Women that he had the "humorous" pleasure of attending. Apparently he derived much of this "whimsical delight" specifically from the appearance of the women asking for the respect due to them as American citizens and human beings. Commenting on one of the speakers, a "severely dressed person from Boston, an old maid from the straightest sect of old maid," Wilson observed that she was a "living example—and lively commentary—of what might be done by giving men's places and duties to women."

Wilson's progressive-minded biographers have tried to offer a defense for the liberal icon's explicit sexism. One wrote, for example, that in his private home Wilson "was unquestionably lord and master, but he ruled with love, and his family literally worshipped him." Of course they worshipped him, they had no choice (although I'm not sure Wilson's biographer knows what "literally" means).

How then, was the same Wilson who wrote in his diary that universal suffrage lay "at the foundation of every evil in this country" accredited as a Democratic president who fought for women's rights? Pure Machiavellian realpolitik. Facing an incredibly close re-election race against Republican candidate Charles Evans Hughes, Wilson was feeling the pressure. His radical progressive agenda was at risk, and he needed votes to keep the liberals' dreams alive. Despite years of pleas from the National American Women Suffrage Association (NAWSA), led by Carrie Chapman Catt, it was only in this moment of desperation that Wilson reluctantly complied and added a women's suffrage plank to the Democratic national platform. Even then though, Wilson rejected the idea of a constitutional amendment to recognize the rights of women across the country. He instead left the question to states like New Jersey, where he had been governor, that continually rejected suffrage referendums. Hughes, representing the GOP as the party that for more than forty years battled against the Democrats to secure the equal rights of citizenship for American women, strongly endorsed a federal amendment.

Catt urged Wilson to do the same, to which he replied, "If I should change my personal attitude now I should seem to the country like nothing better than an angler for votes." One could say that's a commendable response, keeping to his principles, principles of refusing to recognize that women deserve the same political rights as men. But feeling the political pressure, he didn't stick to his sexist beliefs for too long. With the election bearing down, Wilson abandoned his states' rights position when speaking to a NAWSA convention. By his clearly political flip-flop, Wilson secured four more years for the progressives when he narrowly defeated Hughes.

The political game-playing and use of the suffrage issue as a pawn in the grand liberal scheme only continued during Wilson's second term. A lack of progress on the federal amendment and continued Democratic resistance in Congress to women's suffrage left the suffragettes feeling duped by Wilson. Angered by Wilson's intransigence, the National Women's Party commenced daily picketing of the White House in January 1917, braving the cold weather to demand the equality owed them while Wilson watched them from the Oval Office, sipping hot tea. Wilson was eventually moved to action, however, by something more than his own political self-interest: the political interests of the Democratic Party and winning future elections.

A House vote on a suffrage amendment, introduced by recently elected Republican Jeannette Rankin herself, was coming up. With suffragettes rightfully flexing their own political muscle on a Democratic Party that continued to deny them basic rights, Representative Jouett Shouse (D-Kan.), a member of the Democratic National Committee, begged Wilson to rebuke anti-suffrage Democrats "for the sake of the party." He feared that Republicans would harp on the issue they had faithfully advanced for over forty years and set back the Left.

The very next day, Wilson welcomed nine Democratic congressmen who had been present for the January 1915 House vote, six of the nine having voted against the suffrage amendment. In what was publicly billed as a "surprise" move, Wilson told the American people that he "frankly and earnestly" advised them to vote in favor of the federal amendment "as an act of right and justice." Of course, Wilson did not do so for the sake of recognizing women's political and civil equality, but to indebt them to a party whose leaders have never had their interests at heart. Just as LBJ did with civil rights.

Wilson's politically expedient flip on women's rights set the tone that continues today in Democrats' war on women. During the 2012 election, the Obama campaign released an advertisement called "the life of Julia." In this sickening portrayal of the federal nanny state, the Obama campaign walked potential voters through the Left's vision for "women's equality." The ad demonstrated how at every stage of her life, from her childhood, to adolescence, to young professional career, to parenthood, to retirement, the Obama welfare state would be there to give her what she needed to be "successful"—if, of course, Julia votes for the Democratic Party.

This is the true war to make women feel dependent on the political success of the Democratic Party and radical liberals. Susan B.

Anthony, who declared, "I declare to you that woman must not depend upon the protection of man, but must be taught to protect herself, and there I take my stand," would have been outraged at the paternalism rampant in the "life of Julia." It's a two-part war—a war waged to make all women subscribe to certain social behavior, involving complete sexual "liberation" and "independence," and a war waged to convince women that the Democratic Party is the party that will give them everything they need to achieve that narrowminded view on life—if they pledge their political allegiance.

This is not about women's rights. It's about political power and the agenda of the Left, and how a radical feminist movement can conveniently fit into that power grab. Erasing the GOP's historical role in women's rights is key because it hides the plain truth of how the Left hijacked the movement and made it something that the original suffragettes never wanted or could imagine.

The suffragettes sought equality under the law and a constitutional understanding of equality of opportunity. Susan B. Anthony, again, a Republican, proclaimed that "suffrage is the pivotal right," and that "there never will be complete equality until women themselves help to make laws and elect lawmakers." Jeannette Rankin argued that "we're half the people; we should be half the Congress." These are the goals that they rightfully sought, and these are the goals that the GOP stood with them on for vote after vote after vote.

What went wrong? When and how was the women's movement radicalized and hijacked, given over to those with alternative agendas? Well, there are many roots, but some are more clarifying than others.

CHAPTER 3

RISE OF THE FEMI-MARXIST

The individual capitalist family structure is a wasteful social form, not healthy for children to grow up in, a trap for women.

—Prairie Fire, *by Bill Ayers*

The National Organization for Women bills itself as "the largest organization of feminist activists in the United States. NOW has 500,000 contributing members and 550 chapters in all 50 states and the District of Columbia."

That definitely sounds impressive, doesn't it? I was even more impressed to learn from the NOW website that "since its founding in 1966, NOW's goal has been to take action to bring about equality for all women." Unless of course you are a woman who happens to be conservative, or capitalist, or ambivalent in any way about gay rights.

Indeed, NOW's goals have gotten more and more ambitious over the years. The group founded on women's equality now seeks to "eradicate racism" and "eradicate homophobia." Nothing wrong with that, but it's a bit of a deviation from their primary mission. Also their solutions to these problems are the typical big-government programs advocated by liberals for decades—which NOW labels its "economic justice" initiatives. Whatever that means.

When I learned that NOW was going to hold its national convention in Chicago in July 2013, I figured that I owed it to readers of this book to go. After all, if I was going to write about how the political left takes advantage of women and manipulates them for political purposes, I needed to see how the nation's "largest organization of feminist activists" fit in.

Before my applying for press credentials for the convention, I came across a NOW newsletter that proclaimed as its goal for the future "to expand and diversify membership in our ongoing efforts to bring different perspectives to the organization." So I was certain they would be happy to welcome me to cover the convention—since I clearly would add diversity and a vastly different perspective.

Instead, just two days before my departure for Chicago, I was informed that despite being a credentialed female member of the press, my press credentials for this conference were denied. "Thank you for your interest in attending this year's NOW conference as a member of the press," a woman named Sarah Coppersmith wrote to me in an email. "However, press credentials for the conference will not be issued to you. We regret any inconvenience this may have caused." No other explanation was offered.

I wrote back to Ms. Smith the following: "As a credentialed female member of the press, I'd like to know why the credential to the conference was denied, especially considering flights and hotel rooms have already been booked. I look forward to your response. Thank you." She never responded.

I was determined to go to the conference anyway. The only way to do that, I surmised, was to do something I never thought I would do: I became a member of the National Organization for Women in the state of Virginia. I even received a card calling me a "member in good standing," signed by President Terry O'Neill herself. (The things I do for my readers.)

When my plane touched down at O'Hare, I wasn't sure what to expect. I knew Chicago was ground zero for radical movements, and the post-1960s feminist movement was no exception. Chicago, after all, was the home of Saul Alinsky and *Rules for Radicals*, Bill Ayers and the Weather Underground, Jeremiah Wright, and of course Barack Obama. I also knew that NOW was one of the loudest, most visible groups at all the Democratic conventions I'd ever observed. When I walked in on the conference at the Hilton in downtown Chicago I expected to see the room filled with young women fighting for their rights. NOW president Terry O'Neill had just been re-elected and said the day before, "When I was elected four years ago, I pledged to modernize the women's movement by tapping into the energy around the country, bringing people together to protect the rights of women on a number of fronts. During my time as president, together we were able to pass the Violence Against Women Act, elect a record number of women to the U.S. Senate and see marriage equality become a reality in a growing number of states. We have made significant progress, but we're not done yet. We still have more to do and will continue taking our message, enthusiasm and woman power to Virginia and New Jersey's upcoming elections, the midterm races in 2014, the presidential election in 2016 and beyond." For the biggest women's group in the country, at their annual convention, I expected a madhouse of nut cases, shrill lesbians, and other assorted loudmouths.

Instead the large room was nearly empty. I only saw clusters of white baby boomers listening to speeches about abortion, fighting patriarchy in America, and running for office as Democrats. The only energy I felt in the room came from the lightbulbs. But here I was—and I intended to get the most out of my visit anyway.

I walked over to the onsite registration table to get my name tag, just across from a handful of exhibitors. On it I simply wrote "Katie" from "Virginia."

I asked about the attendance. Maybe there had been a bomb scare or maybe I was in the wrong place. There had to be some sort of explanation.

"We expected a couple hundred to show up but it's only been a few dozen," the guy checking me in at the registration table said, looking as if he really missed being at Woodstock. After paying my conference fee, I headed over to the exhibits.

The first table that caught my eye had numerous highlighter orange stickers, posters, and T-shirts. I also came across a table full of classic feminist bumper stickers that made clear NOW's real priorities:

- Hillary 2016
- Women for Democrats
- Against abortion? Don't have one
- The death penalty is dead wrong
- Just say no to sex with pro-lifers
- Explain to me again why I need a man

The only sticker that made any sense to me said, "Real women drive trucks." But I don't think that was meant to appeal to me and my fellow Arizonans, but rather to butch lesbians. Another exhibitor had the January 2009 inaugural issue of *Ms.* magazine (I didn't realize they still published it) with President Barack Obama on the cover wearing a shirt that said, "This is what feminism looks like."

After browsing through the entire exhibit area, which didn't take long due to its being so small, I headed over to the afternoon break-out session and listened to panelists urging women to run as Democrats. In the NOW welcome packet, President O'Neill predictably complained about the ongoing war on women from the right, while ignoring the glorification of those engaged in patriarchy on her side of the aisle. "Despite our extraordinary gains in the 2012 elections, right-wing legislators have not moderated their war on women, and it is more important than ever for women—and men—to join together to defeat their extremist agenda." So much for diversity.

The whole place had the feel of yesteryear. There was singing for the Equal Rights Amendment and chanting of "ERA! ERA!" that hasn't stopped since 1982. The Friday keynote was delivered by the Reverend Jesse Jackson, such a pillar of women's rights that he once stole five hundred thousand dollars from a nonprofit organization in order to pay off his mistress and cover up evidence of their love child.

Perhaps the greatest energy I encountered emanated from the Socialist Party of America, whose volunteers were selling books about Marxism and the feminist movement. I saw another bumper sticker reading "Abortion on Demand and Without Apology!" At the bottom was the name of a website I'd never heard of called "StopPatriarchy.org." Along with the usual call to abort babies proudly and whenever possible, the website offered a prominent link to another site: "Read ongoing coverage & revolutionary analysis of this movement at Revcom.us." Revcom.us is the home of the "Revolutionary Communist Party USA"—where American capitalists are still the enemy, where one article is headlined, "Why I'm A Godless

Communist and Why You Should Be One Too!" and where marriage between a man and a woman is enslavement. As one section of the website states:

> ...the wedding day—now built up into lunatic proportions in countries like the U.S.—marks the passage of a woman into what is all too often a lifetime of domestic drudgery and subordination, whether or not she also works outside the home and very often even if she has an advanced education and a position in a prestigious profession.

When any conservative organization, such as CPAC, even has exhibitors that the mainstream media deems radical, this leads to any number of headlines and news stories designed to embarrass the entire conservative movement. By contrast, when the nation's largest women's rights group features exhibitors that preach Marxist ideologies and condemn American capitalism, there is no comment about it anywhere.

But in fact Marxist teaching is not a tiny fringe part of the modern, militant feminists' agenda. It is its centerpiece.

From the time of Karl Marx through the 1960s and up until today, the progressive women's rights movement has hardly been about women's rights at all but instead about a transformation of American society and the transfer of wealth through government force. Women's rights have simply acted as a veil to distract away from the true intentions of progressive activists. The socialist revolution in America depended on two things: a breakdown of the family and women voting for progressives.

In their 1974 manifesto, *Prairie Fire: The Politics of Revolutionary Anti-Imperialism*, domestic terrorists Bill Ayers, Bernardine Dohrn, and the Weather Underground devoted an entire chapter to how the women's rights movement should be used to advance "revolutionary" goals. Calling feminists to join their ranks and political agenda, they wrote:

> Sexism will not be destroyed until imperialism is overthrown. It is in the collective interests of women to do this and take full part in building a socialist revolution. *We need power* [emphasis added]. Socialist revolution lays the foundation for the liberation of women and begins dismantling the tenacious institutions of sexism.

Only a few hundred copies of *Prairie Fire* were produced, and the book has long been out of print. Only the most committed activists were privileged to see the blueprint of their plans for women and their movement while they moved forward through the decades. As the introduction to the manifesto states, it was written to "communist-minded people," but more important, it was written to women's groups and laid the groundwork for a long-term takeover of the feminist movement. "This analysis represents the beginning of a process, not its final conclusion," they wrote.

In the manifesto, Ayers gave women a set of tasks based on his realization of the power an uprising of women could bring to the progressive cause. "Our goal is the development of feminism which genuinely determines safeguards and defends the collective interests of women, and which points in the direction of revolution. We need to build a revolutionary feminism," Ayers wrote. "Women are at the intersection of the crisis and will fight to survive."

Ayers and his underground believed men acted as male supremacists to women and that in order to change society, a breakdown in the traditional family structure was necessary. In order to destroy that structure, they portrayed women as victims inside it.

"The individual capitalist family structure is a wasteful social form, not healthy for children to grow up in, a trap for women. It is a sanctioned form for sexual exploitation and a hypocritical double standard. The family breeds competitiveness among us, allows no future to women with grown children, and demeans old women, separating them from the life of the community. The ability of single mothers to work and raise and care for children and maintain a household is a monument to women's strength and determination," they wrote on the condition of women. "The modern male-run nuclear family, when we tear away the veil of sentimentality, is the basic unit of capitalist society. Capitalism and the modern family matured together historically, feeding off each other's development."

In reality, a monogamous relationship is anything but sexually exploitative. The principles of monogamy are based on mutual respect, commitment, trust, care, and comfort in order to protect a significant other. It also makes it more likely that older women will be loved and cared for by family members, rather than being shoved into community homes that often include gross abuses of the elderly. Despite what the Weather Underground and their ilk want women to think about the so-called wasteful structure of the free-market economy, the embrace of the traditional family structure is one of the best things to ever happen to women and has kept them out of poverty.

It should be no surprise that, according to a report from the United Nations Development Project,[1] women living in anti-free-market or socialist systems, especially in Eastern Europe, experience higher rates of poverty. In addition, single motherhood in these countries and in the United States has increased poverty among single, working women, limiting their freedom and economic opportunities. Further, a Cambridge University study[2] found single mothers were twice as likely as married mothers to find themselves experiencing financial difficulty, regardless of full-time employment. The study also found single mothers are twice as likely to be depressed. In the United States, 4.1 million single mothers are living in poverty, according to the census.

This 1974 *Prairie Fire* manifesto wasn't on the fringe of far-left policy positions. Its philosophies were deeply embedded in Marxist and socialist thought and are prevalent throughout Marxist and socialist literature. Take, for example, *Feminism and the Marxist Movement: How winning the liberation of women is inseparably linked to the struggle of the working class to transform all economic and social relations*, by Mary-Alice Waters, from 1972. Waters was the editor of the Marxist journal of politics and theory *New International* and idolizes mass murderer Che Guevara in her writings. In her work, Waters details the role socialism played in the stoking of 1960s revolutionary feminism and how the Socialist Workers Party and Young Socialist Alliance promoted the idea of women's liberation being necessary to change the economic structure of the United States.

"We threw ourselves into the movement, to learn from it, to better understand it, to help lead it in an independent and fighting direction, and win the most conscious feminists to an understanding that only a socialist revolution could provide the necessary material foundations for the complete liberation of women," Waters wrote. "At the same time, we began the process of arming ourselves theoretically. We studied the relevant Marxist classics more deeply than before and tried to apply them to current reality. We grounded our practice and political orientation in the fundamentals of Marxism."

Marx was a hero for Waters, someone whom she glorified for pointing out the so-called oppression of women inside the family.

She lamented the idea that many women choose to stay home in the capacity of wife and mother and acknowledged the women's suffrage movement was not built on the idea of destroying capitalism, something that needed to be changed through the hijacking and renaming of the women's "liberation" movement after the 1960s.

As socialists began to infiltrate and hijack the feminist movement, they began to create new organizations parading as women's rights groups with an underlying agenda of socialism and a redistribution of wealth in America. The National Organization for Women, founded on October 29, 1966, was one of those groups and is still active today in shaping public policy in Washington, D.C. Other influential groups included the Women's Radical Action Project, Female Liberation, Chicago Women's Liberation Union, New York Radical Women, and the Women's Liberation Coalition.

Socialist literature sold at the annual NOW conference declares the family system as the origin of female oppression and lays out half a dozen fundamental "errors" of the family.

"Closely intertwined with the origins and character of women's oppression is the question of the family. The resolution reaffirms that the family system is an indispensable pillar of class rule. It is the historical mechanism for institutionalizing the social inequality that accompanies the rise of private property and perpetuating class divisions from one generation to the next," the *Education for Socialists* says. "Because the family system is indispensable to the structuring of social inequality, the economic dependence of women and their oppression within the family system is likewise indispensable to class rule."

Further, this material states Marxists are "the only ones who have answers to the very fundamental questions posed by the feminist movement," and that the answers must be perpetuated through women's liberation literature.

It's no surprise that Marxist materials are available at NOW conferences. The organization was co-founded by Betty Friedan, whose radical leftist roots were central to the group's creation. Before becoming active in the women's liberation movement, Friedan promoted a radical labor-union agenda through her writings for the Federated Press and the *UE News*, the publication of the massive United Electric union. Friedan used the *UE News* to offer conspiratorial reporting, drawing parallels between the 1940s United States and 1940s and 1930s Nazi Germany in terms of worker exploitation and hostility toward unions.[3] Throughout this period, Friedan immersed herself in the world of the radical American left that prompted the Red Scare. As one of her leftist biographers discovered in his research, Friedan and her circle of friends "considered themselves in 'the vanguard of the working-class revolution,' participating in 'Marxist discussion groups,' going to political rallies, and having 'only contempt for dreary bourgeois capitalists like our fathers.'" As Friedan described herself at the time, she was "very involved, consciously radical."[4]

She was not alone. Raya Dunayevskaya, a Russian Marxist activist and progressive feminist hero born in 1910, published *Marxism & Freedom* in 1958. Twenty-six years later, Dunayevskaya published *Women's Liberation and the Dialects of Revolution*, in which she nostalgically remembered the Marxist influence of the feminist liberation movement throughout the 1960s and 1970s and gives credit to NOW for being the "grandmother" of all women's liberation groups.

"It was this aspiration, not only for a particular type of freedom, but for total liberation, that enunciated a new stage of the consciousness of freedom. It is in this sense that the American woman has suddenly begun speaking of her enslavement," she wrote, adding that the aim was for a completely new society. "Private property, Marx insisted, has made us so stupid that we only think of possessions. We are constantly substituting a 'to have' for a 'to be.' But the abolition of private property would not, alone, bring about a new society, as the vulgar communists thought; this, Marx insisted, only 'negates the personality of man,' not to mention the most fundamental of all relations, that of man to woman."

So we know what Waters and Dunayevskaya said about Marx, but what did Marx say about women? It can all be found in his *Communist Manifesto*, in which he boldly states his goals of destroying the family and promoting single women in addition to dependence on an all-powerful state.

"Abolition of the family!" Marx wrote, claiming men exploit their wives for their own personal gain. "On what foundation is the present family, the bourgeois family, based? On capital, on private gain. In its completely developed form this family exists only among the bourgeoisie. But this state of things finds its complement in the practical absence of the family among the proletarians and in public prostitutions."

Marx actually believed keeping women and children protected inside the family was exploitation. He believed they should instead belong to, be raised by, and be educated by the state. "Do you charge us with wanting to stop the exploitation of children by their parents?" he wrote. "To this crime we plead guilty. But, you will say, we destroy the most hallowed of relations when we replace home education by social."

MARRIED TO THE STATE

What Marx failed to mention was how his goals would leave more women and children in poverty. The benefits of marriage for women are great. Not only does marriage decrease the chance of poverty for their children by 82 percent,[5] it also makes women less dependent on the state for help and basic services such as food and medical care, which is exactly the opposite of what progressives want for women.

Since the launch of the failed War on Poverty by Lyndon B. Johnson in 1964 and the degrading of marriage by socialist progressives (as planned by activists like the Weather Underground), we've seen single motherhood rapidly skyrocket. In 1964, just 7 percent of children were born to unmarried parents. Today, that number is 48 percent. In the African-American community, 72 percent of children are born to single mothers. Today, the children of single moms are four times more likely to be poor than children in two-parent homes.[6]

As a result, we've seen the government step in to do the job marriage used to do: nurture, care, and provide. In return, loyal single mothers (and single women) vote to reward big-government providers. The decline of marriage has had big payoffs for Democrats over the past fifty years, because for many people, the benefits of marriage have been replaced by the entitlements of the state defended by Democrats.

Think progressives aren't *really* trying to replace marriage with the state? Think again. Obamacare, one of the largest government takeovers of the American economy and the closest road to socialized medicine in U.S. history, includes a massive marriage penalty.

In January 2010 the Heritage Foundation identified a series of fines for married couples that were part of Obamacare's profound "anti-marriage bias." The Heritage study says Obamacare "profoundly discriminates against married couples, providing far less support to a husband and wife than to a cohabiting couple with the same income." As a result, married couples "will be taxed to provide discriminatory benefits to couples who cohabit, divorce, or never marry." The marriage penalty is about ten thousand dollars per year, per couple in some cases. That amounts to more than two hundred thousand dollars over the lifetime of an average marriage:[7]

> The bill's anti-marriage penalties occur because of the income counting and benefit structure rules of the bill. If a two-earner couple is married, the bill counts their income jointly; since the joint income will be higher, a married couple's health care subsidies would be lower.
>
> By contrast, if a couple cohabits rather than marrying, the bill counts each partner's income separately. Separate counting means that, all else being equal, cohabiters would be treated as having lower incomes and therefore receive disproportionately greater government benefits. The bottom line: under the bill, a cohabiting couple would receive substantially higher health-care subsidies than a married couple even when the total incomes of both couples are identical.

In effect, people get a bonus for avoiding marriage and commitment, which in turn breaks down the traditional family structure.

"The Senate health care bill sends a clear message: Married couples are second-class citizens. On the other hand, the bill establishes cohabiters as a privileged special interest, quietly channeling tens of thousands of dollars to them in preferential government bonuses," Heritage senior research fellow Robert Rector concludes in his analysis of the law.

Offering couples massive financial rewards on the condition they jettison their wedding vows, or decline to make them in the first place, is absurd social policy. In addition, the already established welfare state has been set up to keep women poor while raising children, in the hopes that they'll vote for Democratic policies promoting more welfare. Take, for example, data produced by Pennsylvania secretary of welfare Gary Alexander, which shows a single mother with two kids is better off making just twenty-nine thousand dollars and taking advantage of government programs rather than climbing the ladder to make sixty-nine thousand dollars in income.

"The U.S. welfare system sure creates some crazy disincentives to working your way up the ladder," says American Enterprise Institute columnist James Pethokoukis. "Benefits stacked upon benefits can mean it is financially better, at least in the short term, to stay at a lower-paying job rather than taking a higher paying job and losing those benefits. This is called the 'welfare cliff.'"[8]

In reality, being married to the state makes women dependent on male-dominated institutions—an ironic twist for feminists. The government is overwhelmingly run by men, both in Congress and in government agencies on a federal and state level. On average, 68 percent of senior-level cabinet positions are held by men, and yet many modern-day feminists are content with allowing government to provide them with all of the goods and services they need, rather than relying on themselves or husbands who actually care about them.

ARE WOMEN HAPPIER?

With an increase in the number of single mothers and the breakdown of the traditional family structure that socialist activists call oppressive for women, are women happier? The answer is no. Most women want good relationships and families that give them stability and support. In fact, studies show depression among women has doubled since the 1970s, and women are "two-and-a-half times more likely than men to suffer from depression, with most cases occurring during the 'reproductive years' between the ages of 16 and 42."[9]

My point is not that women were better off in the 1950s, when it was harder to work outside the home. Most women want and deserve a free-market system that allows them to make their own choices about whether to work outside or inside the home. The problem is that Marxist-inspired policies have chipped away at the traditional family structures that must remain viable if women (and men) are going to have a true choice about where to work. Those policies represent the true war on women. Instead, American women have been told Republicans are their true enemies, while they coddle and excuse leftist men who come before them in glamorous packaging. This hypocrisy reached its most ridiculous heights with the Kennedys of Massachusetts, whose women often ended up drunk, or victimized, or dead. The real history of the modern Democratic Party begins with them.

Part II

PROFILES IN LIBERAL MISOGYNY

CHAPTER 4

CRETINS OF CAMELOT

The Senate's strongest advocate for women's rights.

—*National Organization for Women, on Ted Kennedy*

As part of my reporting duties, I was one of the unlucky ones who had to watch much of the 2012 Democratic National Convention. On the evening of September 4, the DNC took seven minutes out of the speaking schedule to show a video titled, *A Tribute to Senator Kennedy*, who had died in 2009 of brain cancer at the age of seventy-seven.

The video, accompanied by flattering images and triumphal music, documented Ted Kennedy's career and private life. Well, parts of it. For some reason the video skipped over one of the most iconic moments of his life: the time when he drove drunk off a bridge, wandered away, and left his twenty-eight-year-old campaign staffer Mary Jo Kopechne to die in his car. No one dared to utter the word "Chappaquiddick" that night, even though the death there almost certainly ended Kennedy's chances to be president of the United States. Instead, the video actually proclaimed Ted Kennedy, who drove his first wife to alcoholism when he wasn't driving other women to drown, a "Champion of Women's Rights." This was put in big, bold lettering on screen. As I watched this, an increasing sense of anger and outrage bubbled up inside me.

Later that night, I was scheduled to participate in a panel discussion on CNN's Piers Morgan program. As I waited in the crowded CNN bar, I watched as Morgan gushed for an entire segment about Ted Kennedy and the wonderful DNC tribute, hoping he would bring it up again when I was on air. Once onstage, I was seated on set next to self-avowed communist Van Jones and just to the right of Democratic strategist and feminist Hilary Rosen, the open-minded, tolerant sort who had infamously said that stay-at-home mother Ann Romney had "never worked a day in her life."

After a few minutes of discussion about the night's speakers, Morgan turned to me. As usual, the media's target that night was not Ted Kennedy and his many sins or the sheer hypocrisy of Obama and other Democrats extolling America's most famous drunk driver. Instead their target was Mitt Romney, who was shown briefly in the video segment expressing a pro-choice position many years earlier.

"Did you feel uncomfortable as a woman watching Mitt Romney, age forty-seven in that Ted Kennedy video, espousing the great joys of pro-choice for women?" he asked in his silky British accent.

This infuriated me even more. "You know what I felt uncomfortable with?" I asked. "That at a convention that stands for women and that is fighting the so-called war on women, that they would pick Ted Kennedy, who left a woman in his car to drown—"

At this point, Hilary Rosen interrupted me. "Oh, stop! Oh, come on."

I continued, "—to be the person in that video. That's how uncomfortable I was."

Morgan, ever the even-handed arbiter of debate and good taste, came down unsurprisingly on Rosen's side. "That's a bit below the belt, I think," said the former editor of one of Britain's most famous trashy tabloids.

Ever the good feminist foot soldier, Rosen immediately shifted the focus from Kennedy's personal war on women to his support for left-wing policies. But she was furious that I dared to point out that Ted Kennedy left the scene of a drowning and thus left a young woman to die.

During the commercial break, she turned to me. "What you said was disgusting."

"I think what he did was disgusting," I responded.

The response from CNN's audience was naturally civil and polite as words like "cunt," "bitch," and "ho" were hurled at me on Twitter. Some suggested "my back should be broke." Viewers also tweeted, "Fuck that bitch that just tried to call out Ted Kennedy on CNN right now. Are you serious?!?!" and, "Who's this crazy chick on CNN that just slandered Ted Kennedy #cnn wow, low blow." Someone operating the @PiersMorganLive account sent out, "Contention among the all-star panel. Katie Pavlich takes heat for Ted Kennedy comment. Live."

I wasn't surprised by the angry, hate-filled reactions. But I was disappointed—disappointed that I couldn't say anything more about the pathetic, terrible, women-hating legacy of America's Worst Family. Any time a Republican says or does anything denigrating women, we are left to hear about it from the media for years—for example, Todd Akin's stupid rape comment, which was used as a metaphor for the entire GOP. Yet somehow when Democrats *actually* use and abuse women, to point out this hypocrisy is somehow "below the belt."

Worse yet are the apologists who say, "Sure, people like Ted Kennedy treat women like dirt in their private lives. But their public policies are good for women." Putting aside the fact their policies hurt women more than they help—as was examined last chapter—the double standard for Democrats and Republicans on this front is astounding. You didn't see liberals giving Clarence Thomas a free pass when he was accused of sexual harassment. They cheered the resignations of Bob Packwood, Newt Gingrich, and Speaker-for-about-a-day Bob Livingston—all brought down by sex scandals.

Most Americans grew up indoctrinated by misty-eyed old leftists like Chris Matthews and others about what a sainted, noble, magical crew the Kennedy family was. Upon JFK's death in 1963, Jacqueline Bouvier Kennedy, JFK's widow/abuse victim, coined the term "Camelot" to describe her husband's administration—a term that came to encapsulate the entire sorry lot. Presumably Mrs. Kennedy meant to conjure notions of royalty, majesty, and glamour. But there's another side of the Camelot story that is much more fitting—of deceit, adultery, dysfunction, illicit love affairs, and illegitimacy.

Despite the pain and humiliation, the Kennedy women have stood by their men for decades, often at tremendous personal cost. Some might call them naïve, others brave soldiers, hoping for the best for their children. Others might say they just stuck it out for the money and power the Kennedy name provided. Generation after generation the Kennedy men have repaid them with even more philandering. What's more, as idolized figures of the Democratic Party, they've set the standard for asinine, misogynistic behavior that is excused, unacknowledged, or erased from history altogether. So let's set the record straight.

KENNEDY CRETIN #1: "THE PATRIARCH"

Joseph P. Kennedy was not content with his humble Irish-American roots in Boston. The man who gifted the world with "America's family" always had higher ambitions—seeking prominent spots in banking, in Hollywood, in the diplomatic service, and most consistently, in beds belonging to anyone other than his long-suffering wife, Rose.

After graduating from Harvard in 1912, Joe Kennedy became the self-proclaimed "youngest bank president" in the United States at twenty-five and immediately set his eyes on other conquests. Where would he find more opportunities for conquest of all sorts than in Hollywood? An outsider set on transforming a massively profitable but very disorganized and disparate film industry, Joe Kennedy made himself right at home and worked hard to craft a powerful image for himself. Featured in *Photoplay* magazine with his wife, Rose, and his seven children, he was extolled as "exceedingly American" and said to come from "a background of lofty and conservative financial connections, an atmosphere of much home and family life and all those fireside virtues of which the public never hears in the current news from Hollywood."[1] It would not take Joe Kennedy very long to debunk those notions.

Joe Kennedy's "hundreds of affairs"—as noted in biographies—would be difficult to cover in this one chapter, or even an entire book. A real Irish charmer, Joe Kennedy had earned a reputation from the early days of his marriage as a "ladies' man," and his letters to male friends and colleagues are full of demands for "good-looking girls" because the "gang around me must be fed on wild meat."[2] This was the attitude that he passed along to his impressionistic sons, and eventually the Democratic Party.

There is perhaps no better place to start understanding the real

Kennedy legacy than with Joe's affair with silent-movie actress Gloria Swanson. After working with her on several films, Kennedy invited Swanson and her third husband, a minor French nobleman, to the Kennedy Palm Beach compound in the winter of 1928. During most winters, Kennedy spent his time playing golf with his millionaire buddies while leaving his wife to tend to mundane matters, such as raising their then seven children. In her 1980 memoir, Swanson tells of "resting in bed" and looking up to see Kennedy rushing at her from her doorway. He kissed her and declared, "No longer, no longer. Now." As she put it, "He was like a roped horse, rough, arduous, racing to be free."

The affair with Swanson began while Rose was in the final months of her pregnancy. Kennedy then did the fatherly thing, returning to Boston to be with his newborn daughter, staying only for a week. Telling Rose that Swanson needed serious financial help that required his immediate attention, he returned to California. Over the long affair, Kennedy became immersed in Swanson's life and that of her children. And he continued to allow himself to be portrayed in the newspapers as a devoted husband, faithful father, and pious Catholic.

Janet Fontaine, one of Joe's secretaries, which almost by definition meant she was also his mistress, said: "He never went to church, I don't think. He never talked about it. He did not go to confession. Oh, God! If a priest heard his confession."[3]

The typical Democratic man, Joe's interest in Swanson faded once he satisfied himself. Swanson's accountant reported that everything Joe had so generously done for her—"the bungalow Kennedy had built for her at Pathé, the mink coat he had 'given' her, along with all the expenses of [the film] *Queen Kelly*"—actually had been billed to Gloria Productions, Swanson's own studio. The expenses were now debts Swanson was solely liable for, upward of a million dollars.[4]

Needless to say, Joe was not exactly the ideal father or role model for his sons, whom he told to get "laid as often as possible."[5] Most horrific, perhaps, was his treatment of his eldest daughter, Rosemary, as biographer Ronald Kessler points out. Unable to tolerate "losers," Joe became increasingly upset with Rosemary because she was slower than the other children and occasionally suffered from fits of violence and anger. His impatience shining once again, he took the advice of two doctors who were major advocates of lobotomy, a horrific and controversial procedure of experimental surgery on the brain. The surgery had terrible effects, and instead of admitting that Rosemary may have been mentally ill before the surgery, Joe decided that it would be better for the family image to say that she was "mentally retarded."[6] Despite the evidence from throughout her life that Rosemary was not mentally retarded, but instead suffered from depression and was made even more ill by the surgery, the family continued to cover up the situation with the blanket statement of mental retardation.

Throughout all of his escapades and all of the examples he set for his children, so that they'd be prepared for American political life, of course, was the stoic mother, Rose Kennedy. Rose's former personal secretary Barbara Gibson told of how "she never showed any pain about those things." Even one step further, Garry Wills described in *The Kennedy Imprisonment* how Rose took great care "not to embarrass the men of the family, obstruct their careers, dim their accomplishments."[7] In other words, Rose Kennedy aided, abetted, and excused her husband's misogyny and thus set the standards for other women in her family to do the same. Just as Democratic women do today for the Kennedys.

KENNEDY CRETIN #2: JOHN FITZGERALD KENNEDY

As a husband, the beloved JFK was a disgrace. "If I don't have sex every day, I get a headache," he once told a member of his cabinet.[8] So he decided not to take any chances.

While his wife exiled herself to the horse country of Virginia, JFK was free to roam the halls of the White House with his hand on his zipper. Affair after affair, some public and others well-kept but well-known secrets, seemed to fill every spare second that JFK was not navigating the United States through one of the most frightening years of the Cold War and the risk of mutually assured destruction.

In July of 1963, FBI Director J. Edgar Hoover called Attorney General Bobby Kennedy to tell him that he knew about the president's past "relationship" with Ellen Rometsch, an alleged East German spy. Rometsch made some money on the side by "working" with Washington elites while her husband was assigned to the West German embassy.[9] A "budding communist" before coming to the United States, Rometsch attended some of JFK's many "naked pool parties" at the White House in the spring of 1963 and showed up explicitly to have sex with the president more than once. Fearing what might happen to his brother's re-election chances (he probably should have been more concerned with national security), Bobby Kennedy reportedly arranged for her to be deported.[10]

When he was not endangering national security, JFK was having a field day endangering his political career. It is hard to tell what's more of a miracle: that America didn't get into a war over the Cuban Missile Crisis or that JFK wasn't chased out of the White House by a mob of angry mistresses.

One of his mistresses was connected to the *actual* mob. Introduced to the president by Frank Sinatra in Las Vegas in 1960, Judith Exner was certainly one of the sketchiest of Jack's "conquests" (if the alleged East German spy wasn't enough). It is believed that she was an active mistress of the president while she also began sleeping with the leader of the Chicago Mafia Sam Giancana and his associate John Roselli. Exner said in her autobiography that "Jack never in a million years thought he was doing anything that would hurt me, but that's the way he conducted himself; the Kennedys have their own set of rules. Jack was reckless, so reckless."[11]

As if Rometch and Exner weren't the most dangerous of Jack's lovers, the actress Marilyn Monroe was invited to Palm Springs a month after the president met her at a dinner party. Of course, as JFK told her on the phone, his wife, Jackie, would not be there. While it's believed that the weekend in Florida was the extent of the affair, it didn't stop Monroe from telling Jackie about it in an attempt to get the president all to herself.

Among the creepiest of Jack's affairs was his relationship with Mimi Alford. The tall and striking Wheaton College co-ed met JFK by chance, and before she knew it, the White House offered her a summer internship that she hadn't even applied for. Mimi soon found out why she'd been hired. In her first week on the job, the nineteen-year-old virgin was led to Jackie's bedroom, where there was nothing "short of screaming" she could do to get the president off her. For the next eighteen months, they had sex "on an Air Force jetliner, in a presidential limousine, on foreign trips, in the White House swimming pool and even in the mansion's upstairs bathtub"— where they had rubber ducky races. Feeling generous, JFK once asked Mimi to have oral sex with his press aide, David Powers: "Mr. Powers looks a little tense," said the thirty-fifth president. "Would you take care of it?"[12]

Alford was not the only mistress on the White House payroll. JFK lobbied Jackie to hire as her personal press secretary Pamela Turnure, who was Jack's press secretary when he was a senator. Of course, Jack's lobbying came with a price: Widely said to be a Jackie Kennedy lookalike, Turnure was expected to sleep with the president on nights that Jackie was traveling.[13]

Two other White House aides, secretaries Priscilla Wear and Jill Cowen, spent so much time with the president instead of doing work that they received the code names: "Fiddle and Faddle." They often joined in threesomes with Jack in the White House pool and were assigned to travel with him despite the absolute irrelevance of their positions to his travel arrangements or foreign policy.[14]

Sometimes, JFK tried to keep it in the family. What better way to solidify a father-son relationship, he must have figured, than to have an affair with the same woman? When Marlene Dietrich was invited to drinks at the White House in September 1963, the president made a "clumsy pass" at the sixty-year-old actress. JFK then questioned her about sleeping with his father, and when she denied the affair, the king of Camelot supposedly responded, "I always knew the son of a bitch was lying." (He wasn't.)[15]

Last in this list of trysts—which is far from exhaustive—is the bizarre case of Mary Pinchot Meyer. A friend of JFK's since high school, Meyer was married to an important CIA agent and was sister-in-law to the editor of the *Washington Post*, putting her in Kennedy's Washington circle. A known mistress who visited him at the White House frequently, Meyer became close with LSD guru Timothy Leary, who claims that he and Meyer were involved in a strange plot to get Washington elites on LSD and thereby bring about peace. Meyer was mysteriously killed execution style in D.C. in October 1964.[16]

This sampling paints the picture of a man who should have been seen as a disgrace to his family, the Democratic Party, and his country. Of course his behavior instead is standard fare for the Democratic elite. Larry Newman, a young agent on Kennedy's security detail, recounted the "morale problems" that the president's indiscretions caused among his fellow Secret Service agents. "You were on the most elite assignment in the Secret Service, and you were there watching an elevator or a door because the president was inside with two hookers. Your neighbors and everybody thought you were risking your life, and you were actually out there to see that he's not disturbed while he's having an interlude in the shower with two gals from Twelfth Avenue."[17] If only the humiliation had ended with the tragedy of JFK's death. Apparently, the Democratic Party didn't want the fun to stop there.

KENNEDY CRETIN #3: ROBERT FRANCIS KENNEDY

Said to be more timid and family oriented than his brothers, it is a shame that Robert F. Kennedy ended up joining the long list of unfaithful Kennedy men.

Rumors continue to abound about RFK's affair with Marilyn Monroe, which would fit perfectly with the perverted Kennedy obsession for the same "conquests." But perhaps what is more revealing and just plain sad is Bobby's alleged four-year affair with Jackie Kennedy after JFK's death. C. David Heymann, investigative writer and author of several best-selling books about the Kennedy family escapades, added a whole new episode to the soap opera in *Bobby and Jackie: A Love Story*. Following her death, Heymann found many confidants willing to tell of the four-year love affair that started far too soon after the assassination of JFK.

The fact that Bobby and his wife, Ethel Skakel, already had eight children seemed of no relevance to the romance that emerged. Taking after his father, Bobby was soon spending more time with Jackie and his nephew and niece than he was with his own family. Two months after returning from vacation in Antigua, where Ethel took her own and Jackie's children skiing, Bobby took the two women on a dinner cruise around the Potomac River on the presidential yacht. Speechwriter Arthur Schlesinger watched Bobby and his sister-in-law disappear below deck alone at one point, and believes it started there.[18] Among the many stories unearthed through his interviews, Heymann describes the experience of Mary Harrington, who lived next door to the Kennedy house in Palm Beach. Harrington says "she observed Jackie sunbathing on the grass, Bobby kneeling by her side, and the two beginning to kiss—and then he placed one hand on her breast and the other inside of her bikini bottom. The couple soon disappeared inside."[19]

It's hard to call the affair a "love story" though, considering the liaisons that both Bobby and Jackie continued during their "romance." Jackie began dating Greek tycoon Aristotle Onassis, who began paying her considerable living expenses. Meanwhile, Bobby had several more affairs, which may have included Mary Jo Kopechne.[20] Her tragic story and abuse is saved for another Kennedy's story.

Choosing denial over confrontation, Ethel Kennedy refused to believe the evidence that was right in front of her eyes. Years after RFK's assassination, she was appalled by friends' recommendation to find another husband. She responded, "How could I possibly do that with Bobby looking down from heaven? That would be adultery."[21]

KENNEDY CRETIN #4: WOMEN'S CHAMPION TED KENNEDY

The National Organization for Women notes proudly on their website that Ted Kennedy's "Senate office was always open to women's rights advocates." Probably because he was looking for dates—not that he'd find most NOW leaders even remotely appealing. "No other member of Congress has achieved so much for women."

The youngest son of Joe Kennedy, Edward "Ted" Kennedy took the reins of victimizing women from his slain elder brothers.

The aforementioned Chappaquiddick incident of course remains the most notorious incident. Hosting a party at his house on Chappaquiddick Island, Senator Ted Kennedy left to "drive home" Mary Jo Kopechne, a 1968 campaign staffer for Robert Kennedy, even though she strangely left her hotel key and purse at the party. Claiming that he was not intoxicated, Kennedy drove his car off a bridge into a tidal pool, before escaping the submerged car. He said he attempted to search for Kopechne multiple times, before leaving the scene and not reporting the incident until the car and Kopechne's body were found. Kennedy served just a two-month sentence for leaving the scene of an accident after causing injury. Announcing the sentence, Judge James Boyle noted Kennedy's "unblemished record."

Perhaps the judge just missed the legal files of Kennedy's record as a law student at the University of Virginia, when he was arrested for reckless driving after a chase with police. The judge further held that Ted "has already been, and will continue to be punished far beyond anything this court can impose." Perhaps the judge thought the incident would doom Ted's political career. It didn't.

The nature of the crime was discovered to be even worse when an autopsy on Kopechne revealed that she had died of asphyxiation in the car, meaning that she had survived the initial crash by breathing in a small air pocket in the submerged car. If Ted had not inexplicably waited nine hours to report the "accident," she might have survived. Mary Jo's mother later said: "I don't think he ever said he was sorry."[22]

Whereas being the cause of an innocent young woman's death might have been reason for a change in lifestyle, Ted Kennedy continued a distinguished career in the Senate while stacking up one outrageous scandal after another while off the job. As Michael Kelly reported in his essay-length exposé of Ted Kennedy for *GQ* magazine, "In Washington, it sometimes seems as if everyone knows someone who has slept with Kennedy, been invited to sleep with Kennedy, seen Kennedy drunk, been insulted by Kennedy."[23]

Stories abound. After a long dinner one night between Kennedy and his friend Democratic senator Chris Dodd at La Brasserie in Washington, D.C., waitress Carla Gaviglio didn't know what she was in for. Before her shift ended, Ted Kennedy had thrown her on a table, a table that became nothing but a chaotic mess of broken plates, spilled hot candle wax, and broken crystal. *GQ*'s Michael Kelly[24] recorded the dirty details from there: "Kennedy then picks her up from the table and throws her on Dodd, who is sprawled in a chair. With Gaviglio on Dodd's lap, Kennedy jumps on top and begins rubbing his genital area against hers, supporting his weight on the arms of the chair. As he is doing this, another waitress enters the room. She and Gaviglio both scream, drawing one or two dishwashers. Startled, Kennedy leaps up. He laughs. Bruised, shaken and angry over what she considered a sexual assault, Gaviglio runs from the room."[25]

The incident was apparently not enough for La Brasserie to put Ted Kennedy on a "sexual predators" list. On September 25, 1987, Kennedy was back with a young blonde woman—identified by several sources as a congressional lobbyist. They allegedly got carried away at a lunch in a private room upstairs and were discovered semi-undressed in the act by a waitress. The bill for the lunch had only two items: two bottles of champagne.[26]

Calls about the senator's behavior became so regular that one Kennedy press secretary reportedly standardized the response for the office: "It is our policy never to comment on this endless gossip and speculation." Gossip and speculation aside, Kennedy had the good sense to lie low when other questionable behavior popped up in the spotlight around him. According to *Time* magazine, Kennedy took a "surprisingly passive role in the 1991 Supreme Court confirmation hearings of Justice Clarence Thomas,"[27] who had been accused of sexual harassment. The same Kennedy who had led the brutal assault against the nomination of conservative Robert Bork a few years earlier hid out of sight, much to the chagrin of his liberal base.[28]

As with most of the delinquent Kennedy men, a brave woman stood beside him, only to fall prey to the poisonous atmosphere around her. Ted's wife, Joan Kennedy, had a few years of happy marriage before the assassinations of John and Robert weighed on the family. The publicity surrounding Chappaquiddick and further revelations of Ted's "apparently relentless skirt chasing" led Joan to alcohol. "Rather than get mad or ask questions concerning the rumors about Ted and his girlfriends, it was easier for me to just go and have a few drinks and calm myself down, as if I weren't hurt or angry."[29] Racked by continual stories of her husband's behavior and the failings of her children, their divorce was followed only by worse bouts of alcoholism for Joan. She quietly attended Ted's funeral, still with little support from her family.

Through all of the skirt chasing and womanizing, the reckless behavior and Chappaquiddick scandal, it is hard to believe a word the man ever said. "I hope for an America where we can all contend freely and vigorously, but where we will treasure and guard those standards of civility which alone make this nation safe for both democracy and diversity." For the sake of everyone, especially women, I hope that Americans never look to Ted Kennedy for our "standards of civility."

THE CIRCUS CONTINUES

"America's family" did not "bury its past" with the loss of its first and second generations. Indeed the next generation of Kennedys has engaged in even more anti-women behavior in what amounts to, in some cases, a crime spree.

In 2012, Mary Kennedy hanged herself in her Westchester garage. She and her husband, Robert Kennedy, Jr., were in the middle of a bitter divorce and child custody battle, which had likely only exacerbated her depression, alcoholism, and financial difficulties. The final straw, however, may have been her discovery of a diary Robert kept in 2001. It detailed a year in the life of a sex addict, describing dozens of women he'd taken to bed.[30]

In the diary, "numbers corresponded to sexual acts, with a ten denoting intercourse. At the back of the diary, in the section marked 'cash accounts,' Kennedy noted the names of all 37 women with whom he cheated on his wife that year—16 of whom got tens."[31]

Even more crass than his philandering was its timing. Neither the birth of Kennedy's fourth child in July, nor the attacks by Al Qaeda in September, slowed down Robert Kennedy, Jr. On November 13, he had three affairs in a single day—only one was "scored" a "ten."[32]

In defense of Robert Kennedy, Jr., at least the prolific philandering he describes in his sex diary was apparently consensual. It's not a safe bet to say the same thing for all sex with Kennedy men. Take, for example, William Kennedy Smith's alleged rape of a young woman on a beach in Miami.

It was the evening of Good Friday, but the Kennedy men were not exactly mourning the passion and suffering of Christ's crucifixion. Instead, Ted Kennedy, his son Patrick, and his nephew William were trolling for women at a bar in Palm Beach. They took two women from the bar to the nearby beach house, and one joined William for a walk on the beach, where, according to her account, he raped her.[33]

At trial, William Kennedy Smith was acquitted, and we may never know what really happened on that beach. But we do know that three other women were willing to testify, and they alleged, and were barred from testifying, that William had sexually assaulted them in prior years.[34] And that a co-worker later sued him for sexual assault. And that he later settled with yet another co-worker over a sexual harassment claim. In one incident of particularly creepy conduct, he was accused of stroking the pregnant woman's stomach and trying to kiss her, before he "inched his hand below her waist, and stuck his tongue in her ear," prompting the object of his affections to rush from the room.[35]

At William Kennedy Smith's rape trial, he had the benefit of a high-priced lawyer, but that wasn't enough for Michael Skakel. Skakel is the nephew of Robert Kennedy's widow, Ethel, and he worked for Ted Kennedy. In 2002, he was convicted of using a golf club to bludgeon to death fifteen-year-old Martha Moxley, who was found dead with her pants and underwear pulled down. Evidence at trial suggested Skakel killed Moxley because she refused to have sex with him. Two former friends testified that Skakel had confessed the murder to them, saying, "I'm going to get away with murder. I'm a Kennedy."

According to Skakel, he didn't kill Martha Moxley; he only masturbated from a tree while trying to peer into the fifteen-year-old's bedroom on the night of the murder. In 2013, after he had served eleven years in prison, Skakel's verdict was overturned based on the dubious claim that he was not adequately represented by his million-dollar legal defense. He will likely face a retrial.[36]

Of course, there are plenty more among the Kennedy clan's third generation of sexual deviants. Robert Kennedy Jr.'s married brother Michael had an affair with a fourteen-year-old babysitter, and it was probably only her unwillingness to cooperate with investigators that saved him from a statutory rape prosecution.[37] Patrick Kennedy was accused by William Kennedy Smith's prosecutors of covering up Smith's alleged rape. And then there's Arnold Schwarzenegger. A Kennedy only by marriage, he impregnated his housekeeper while married to Maria Shriver, Joseph Kennedy Sr.'s granddaughter. Another woman said Schwarzenegger once "pulled her onto his knee, circled her left nipple with his finger and he asked her if her breasts were real."[38] It turns out that the action hero, governor, and Kennedy-by-marriage had a history of sexually harassing and assaulting women.

Joseph Kennedy would be proud.

CHAPTER 5

BILL CLINTON, FATHER OF THE YEAR

I ask that all Americans demonstrate in their personal and public lives . . . the high ethical standards that are essential to good character and to the contin- ued success of our Nation.

—Accused serial sexual assaulter Bill Clinton, 1997

As Hillary Rodham Clinton seeks the White House again, there is an active effort underway to whitewash, ignore, excuse, or explain away the real Clinton record, especially when it comes to women. I say, not so fast.

There's one thing liberal women seem to never get sick of: liberal men treating their gender poorly. This couldn't have been more clear than when former president Bill Clinton was named "Father of the Year" in 2013 by the National Father's Day Council—an organiza- tion that also named JFK a father of the year in 1963—and women's groups responded with silence, or even cheers. Renowned feminist- of-convenience Hillary Clinton said the award was well-deserved. Surprise, surprise.

If a conservative with a record of alleged rapes and sexual assaults had been given the award, women's rights groups would have howled in protest. If a conservative forty-eight-year-old employer had used his power and his office to seduce a twenty-two-year-old intern—in the same house where his fifteen-year-old daughter slept—feminists would have united in objection. Instead, groups like NOW and NARAL reserved their ire for Republicans like Bob Packwood and Republican-appointed judges like Clarence Thomas, on the grounds that Clinton was different because his "policies" supported women.

A closer look at those policies shows that there was nothing particularly pro-women about them. Clinton used his abortion position to claim he was in favor of women being in control of their medical decisions, but if he had his way, they might not have been able to even pick their own doctors. Clinton pushed for Hillarycare, which would have made Obamacare look like only a minor tweaking of the health-care industry, and the only thing that stopped him was a congressional coalition of conservatives and moderate Democrats (yes, they used to exist).

Clinton's policies also punished female entrepreneurs, small business owners, and working moms. His bureaucrats burdened them with regulations. His environmental policies made it harder for female developers, especially in the West. And he imposed on female taxpayers the largest tax increase in American history.

Of course, Clinton's behavior toward women in private was even more atrocious than his public policies. One can only imagine, while Bill Clinton was receiving his father of the year award, how all the fathers of all his mistresses felt about the former commander in chief. It's easy to forget that women like Monica Lewinsky and Paula Jones had fathers, too, and they surely didn't enjoy seeing their daughters' names dragged through the mud by their association with the sex-crazed womanizer in the White House.

Many abusers like to denounce behavior committed by others that parallels their own. During the course of his affair with Monica, Clinton would make statements about older men preying on younger women, as he did during a speech on teen pregnancy in 1996. "The other thing we have to do is to take seriously the role in this problem of older men who prey on underage women," he said. He added, without a hint of irony, "There are consequences to decisions and . . . one way or the other, people always wind up being held accountable."

Shortly after Clinton was busted by Matt Drudge for having sexual relations with an intern in the Oval Office, pundits took to the airwaves to discuss how this would affect the remainder of his time in the White House and his place in history. One of his most virulent defenders was Ann Lewis, communications director of the Clinton White House and the sister of sanctimonious ultraliberal Barney Frank. Ms. Lewis proclaims herself a devoted feminist. As Christopher Hitchens recollected in his excellent book on the Clintons, *No One Left to Lie To*, Lewis found men so repugnant that "she could not approve any presidential utterance that used 'man' to mean 'mankind.'"

Yet the same Ms. Lewis was such a proud defender of women's rights that she was at the forefront of efforts to defend Clinton against multiple allegations that he assaulted women (including one instance when he was accused of rape) and multiple stories of humiliating his wife and daughter with his endless quest for a quick lay.

She loved defending a president so uncontrollably obsessed with sex that he was known to doodle sexually explicit pictures on national security documents. On a document that included the text, "This plan may not be attractive to Milosevic, who has indicated to negotiators that he wants near-total sanctions relief," Clinton drew an erect penis.

To be sure, there were women during the Clinton presidency who knew he wasn't the champion of women he claimed to be. *Washington Post* reporter Nina Burleigh, who wrote an entire book about the 1964 murder of President John F. Kennedy's mistress Mary Meyer, revealed[1] in 1995 that when it came to respecting and promoting women, Clinton overpromised and underdelivered:

> The progressive Bill Clinton appears amply willing to promote women's interests, having put more females in political appointments than any president in history. But Bill Clinton the "good ol' boy" seems by his behavior to have an indifferent personal attitude toward females.
>
> For those women closest to Clinton, the evidence is everywhere. Inside the White House, top-level women have been shut out of the inner circle, snubbed and given titles without responsibility. Many have had difficulty doing their job because they aren't kept in the loop. Others complain about the lack of access they have to Clinton, or of finding out about meetings they should have been in long after they're over.

Despite writing about Clinton's use of women as political props to win votes and to make it look like he actually cares, Burleigh would later make one of Bill Clinton's most vulgar and hyperbolic defenses. In 1998, when what Bill Clinton left on Monica Lewinsky's dress was being examined by the special prosecutor, she said, "I would be happy to give [Bill Clinton] a blow job just to thank him for keeping abortion legal. I think American women should be lining up with their presidential kneepads on to show their gratitude for keeping the theocracy off our backs."[2]

When I reached out to Ms. Burleigh recently about her comments, she referred me to a series of essays on her website and on the *Huffington Post*. In those essays, written nearly ten years after her infamous remarks about kneepads, the same woman who supported a president preying on an intern half his age blamed conservative men for just not understanding what true sexual harassment really is:[3]

> I said it (back in 1998, but a good quote has eternal life) because I thought it was high time for someone to tweak the white, middle-aged Beltway gang taking Clinton to task for sexual harassment. These men had neither the personal experience nor the credentials to know sexual harassment when they saw it, nor to give a good goddamn about it if they did. The insidious use of sexual harassment laws to bring down a president for his pro-female politics was the context in which I spoke.

In other words, she proved my point. As long as he's a liberal, a man can use the power of his position to put women into any position he wants. Burleigh exemplifies how Bill Clinton was able to get away with repeated bad behavior: Liberal women allowed him to. *Good Morning America* co-host Lisa McRee said in 1998: "Women who've been polled seem to put it behind them as well, and are willing to move on and forget about it. Is that because Bill Clinton's been such a great president whom they elected in great part, or is there something I want to say almost sexy about a man who can get away with things over and over again?"

McRee was certainly right about one thing: Bill Clinton was able to "get away with things over and over again." Time and again, he used women for sex, and when he was caught, the creep turned around and lied about it while smearing the women he preyed on.

This was the case with former television reporter and cabaret singer Gennifer Flowers, whose relationship with Clinton was exposed in 1992 when he was running for the White House. In an effort to get ahead of the story, Bill and Hillary sat down with reporter Steve Kroft on *60 Minutes* to try and lie their way out of the scandal.

The interview was textbook Clinton. He called Flowers merely "a friendly acquaintance." He called the allegation of a "twelve-year affair" with her "false." He said she'd been driven to lie when "the tabloid went down there offering people money." He admitted "causing pain in my marriage," but then he quickly turned from self-reflection to self-pity: "I have said things to you tonight and to the American people from the beginning that no American politician ever has." (Most of them don't have to.) Finally, he went on the attack, against the media: "I think what the press has to decide is: Are we going to engage in a game of 'gotcha'?"

Finally, the coup de grace came from Hillary, who combined the invitation for pity with the attack on the press. "There isn't a person watching this," she pleaded, "who would feel comfortable sitting on this couch detailing everything that ever went on in their life or their marriage. And I think it's real dangerous in this country if we don't have some zone of privacy for everybody." As they would do again and again over the years, the Clintons turned the matter into an attack on their privacy rather than on their dishonesty with the American people.

Six years after the *60 Minutes* interview and from a secure place in the White House, Clinton finally admitted he in fact did have an affair with Flowers back in 1977 (although he claimed, dubiously, that it only happened "once"). In the meantime, Flowers had been portrayed as a harlot, a bimbo, a trashy liar willing to sell a false story for a couple of bucks.

Based on that portrayal, few people would think of Gennifer Flowers as a feminist, but when I took the time to actually interview Flowers, I found someone who is the definition of what the feminist movement of the 1960s and 1970s described as a liberated woman. She's independent, beautiful, has lived a life providing for herself, and is open and comfortable with her sexuality. She strongly believes she has a right to her thoughts, needs, beliefs—a right to equality, equal pay, getting ahead based on hard work, and competing against women and men. She was a proud part of the bra-burning, sexually active, women's liberation movement. "It was just like the world opened up," Flowers told me, referring to the women's liberation movement. "I was one of the first ones there, I loved it. I thought it was fantastic."

Flowers started her life as an entertainer and local television reporter at a time when women were not welcome at the anchor desk. She told me, "The old anchor guy said, 'I'm not going to co-anchor with a man, much less a woman.' Every guy in there was trying to get in my britches. They didn't want to take me seriously." She adds, "I have gone through a great deal as a woman, an independent woman, a liberated woman, that has very definitive views and opinions, and it's not been easy."

As part of her embrace of the women's liberation movement, Flowers also believes in abortion rights, and she's been frank about the abortion she had after becoming pregnant with what she said was Bill Clinton's child.

"When I told Bill I was pregnant, stupid me, I thought if ever there's a time that he's going to make the decision to get a divorce and that we can be together it's now," Flowers recalls. "He said, 'Well, I'd be glad to help.'" By "help," Clinton meant he would help pay for Flowers's abortion. According to his mistress, he reached into his wallet, pulled out two hundred-dollar bills, and handed them over. Flowers remembers that she thought, "You're on your own with this, Gen, and you've got a decision to make."

When the news broke in 1992 that Flowers was engaged in an affair with then Arkansas governor Bill Clinton, her dedication to and perception of the so-called feminist movement completely changed. "I thought that when his group started calling women bimbos and trailer trash and a variety of things, I thought that I would get support from women's groups that are typically Democratic in my opinion based on the abortion issue, generally." Instead, Flowers learned that "these women had their agenda," and if you "don't fit into it," then "they're not going to support you."

After Flowers told the story of her affair with Bill Clinton, Clinton's misogynist mafia of James Carville, George Stephanopoulos, and other political hacks kicked into gear. When it came to women Clinton had been involved with, the mission was simple: Discredit them and make them look unbelievable. "He had his spin doctors and his war room who were put in place to do nothing but destroy women," Flowers says. "They bragged about it."

Clinton's betrayal of Flowers went beyond denying their more-than-a-decade-long affair and the decision to abort a child. "My home was entered and ransacked before the story became public," she says. "It was entered three times, the third time it was ransacked."

When Flowers called Clinton, she says he told her, "Don't call the police."

"Well, what do you expect me to do?" Flowers said.

"Well, do you think they were looking for something on us?" Clinton allegedly asked.

Flowers then thought, "You had this done." She knew Clinton had a key to her apartment, which was easy to duplicate, and she says of her suspicion that he had hired someone to destroy her apartment and take any information indicating an affair, "I mean, I knew this man, I could tell." (Years later, the home of another Clinton accuser named Kathleen Willey would allegedly be burglarized. According to Willey, the only item stolen was a manuscript of her book about Bill and Hillary Clinton.)

Flowers's hatred of Clinton's minions—such as those she believed had broken into her apartment—intensified when she saw how they attacked former Arkansas state clerk Paula Jones, who claimed Clinton forced himself on her and demanded oral sex in a suite at the Excelsior Hotel during a conference in 1991. Flowers watched on television as all the usual suspects did exactly what they always do. Clinton denied even knowing Jones, and James Carville quipped, "Drag a hundred-dollar bill through a trailer park, you never know what you'll find."

"Let me tell you who responds to a hundred dollars being dragged through any place," Flowers told me. "It's that sorry SOB. You think he was getting out there for nothing? And acting that way and treating women that way? Do you think he was doing it because he just wanted to? No, he did it because he was getting paid well and has no respect and regard for women."

When Carville slandered Paula Jones, Flowers held out hope that the women's groups that had failed to defend her would at least support Jones. Sure, maybe feminists believed consensual sex should stay private, but they'd spent their lifetimes railing against the kind of illegal sexual harassment Jones was alleging. "I expected them to get pissed off at us being pigeonholed as 'bimbos,' 'trailer trash,' and 'low-down whores,'" Flowers says. When they didn't, she recalls, "My whole image was just crushed of what I thought, I really honestly thought that they were going to come out with signs and force against the way we were being treated as women. . . . That shattered my image and certainly I had no respect any longer for those groups."

The outrage boiling inside Flowers reached a peak during the Lewinsky scandal. "I'll tell you what, he's lucky Monica Lewinsky wasn't my daughter. To be at the White House as an intern, what an incredible experience, she's supposed to be in a safe environment and taken care of and respected and I'm not saying that she didn't do anything wrong but he was the role model, he was the adult, and the president of the United States takes a young girl into the Oval Office giving him blow jobs and screwing her with a cigar? Are you kidding me? Who does that not offend?"

The answer to her last question is, apparently, the groups that claim to represent women and defend their interests—the very groups that rallied to Clinton's defense. "As women, we were getting used," says Flowers. "We were getting used and screwed and not kissed by the Democrats again. By the Bill Clintons and the Ted Kennedys, all these men that have victimized women."

The most injured of those victims may have been two women who accused Bill Clinton of some of the most heinous sexual behavior ever said to have been committed by him—which, in light of cigars and sexual harassment and burglary, is really saying something.

The first woman was a former nurse named Juanita Broaddrick. She served as a volunteer for Clinton's gubernatorial campaign, and one day, Clinton asked to meet with her. Initially, they agreed to meet in her hotel's coffee shop, but Clinton called and asked to meet in her room due to reporters' being in the lobby. With hesitation, she agreed and set up coffee near the window. When Clinton came into the room there was a brief conversation before he started kissing her. When she resisted, he got violent, bloodying her lip and tearing her panty hose. Then, according to Broaddrick, Bill Clinton raped her.

A similar story was recounted in the 1990s by Kathleen Willey, a self-described strong Democrat and loyal supporter of the Clintons. She later wrote in her book *Target: Caught in the Crosshairs of Bill and Hillary Clinton* about being sexually assaulted by Bill Clinton in the Oval Office after telling him about an emergency financial situation with her husband.

I turned and went through the small hallway toward the Oval Office and President Clinton followed closely behind me. When I turned around at the end of the small hallway, he was right next to me. He expressed his regret for my situation and gave me a big hug, but his hug lasted a little too long. I pulled back. All of a sudden, he was running his hands in my hair and around the back of my neck.

What the hell?

He kissed me on my mouth and, before I knew it, I was back up in to the corner, against the closed bathroom door and the wall behind the Oval Office. The president's hands were all over me, just all *over* me. And all I could think was, *What the hell is he doing? Just what is he doing?*

I tried to twist away. He was too powerful. President Clinton is almost a foot taller than I am and nearly double my weight. I couldn't get away and could barely think. I didn't know what I was supposed to do. He was my friend. And he was the president of the United States.

I finally managed to say, "What are you doing?"

"I've wanted to do this," he said, "since the first time I laid eyes on you."

What?

I was terrified for my husband, for my family, for our future, and the president says he's wanted to do this since he laid eyes on me? I was totally unprepared for that.

Then he took my hand. I didn't understand what he was doing. The president put my hand on his genitals, on his erect penis. I was shocked! I yanked my hand away but he was forceful. He ran his hands all over me, touching me everywhere, up my skirt, over my blouse, my breasts. He pressed up against me and kissed me. I didn't know what to do. I could slap him or yell for help. My mind raced. And the only thing I noticed was that his face had turned red, literally beet red.

Had he the opportunity—the time and the privacy—I believe Clinton would have raped me that day, just as, I believe, he raped Juanita Broaddrick.

Kathleen Willey was dismissed by liberals and quickly forgotten by the media. The problem wasn't what she was claiming; it was who she was accusing. Liberals weren't interested in holding Clinton and Democrats accountable for their conduct toward women. They only wanted to hold Republicans accountable, as the March 17, 1998, issue of the *New York Times* showed:[4]

> Despite the new outspokenness among some, most women Democrats on Capitol Hill were still reluctant to come forward with a united front as they did against Republican figures who had been accused of sexual harassment, including Clarence Thomas during his confirmation hearings for the Supreme Court, and former Senator Bob Packwood of Oregon.
>
> As an example, Geraldine Ferraro, who is seeking the Democratic nomination for Senate from New York, said she was out to

dinner Sunday night and missed *60 Minutes* but had no interest in seeing a tape of Ms. Willey's interview.

"I haven't gotten the tape of Paula Jones, so why would I get the tape of this?" she asked in an interview. "I can't assess what's real and what's not real. And I don't want to."

Senator Barbara Boxer of California, who is seeking re-election this year, also chose not to take a stand, saying: "Ms. Willey has made serious charges and they deserve to be thoroughly investigated. It should also be noted that the President has unequivocally denied these charges."

Senator Trent Lott of Mississippi, the Republican leader, today castigated women's organizations for their "deafening silence."

Lott was hardly at the cutting edge of women's rights and civil rights. He famously said that America wouldn't have "all these problems" if the Dixiecrat Strom Thurmond had been elected president in 1948. But what does it say about the women's rights movement that Trent Lott did a better job in the late 1990s standing up for the sexually harassed and assaulted than did NOW and women's groups like it?

"I wonder where are the women's voices and where are the Democratic colleagues that must be feeling some sense of outrage about what is going on here?" Mr. Lott asked. "If we don't hear more out of them after the Kathleen Willey statement on Sunday night, then I can't guess we'll ever hear from them again."

To this day, their silence, like their hypocrisy, continues.

CHAPTER 6

THE CLINTON DEMOCREEPS

I'm not sure it rises—no pun intended—to that level.

—*Congressman Anthony Weiner, on whether he would press criminal charges against the person he claimed hacked his Twitter account*

In 2010, Rob Ford was elected mayor of Toronto, Ontario. Over the years, Ford had built a colorful record of public service. Ford had dismissed women with AIDS—"How are women getting it?" he once asked. "Maybe they are sleeping with bi-sexual men."—and said "Oriental people work like dogs" and are "slowly taking over."[1] Ford survived a 1999 arrest for DUI and marijuana possession and a conflict of interest trial. The public had even forgiven him for shouting so many obscenities at a couple at a Maple Leafs hockey game that Ford was escorted from the game by security guards.[2] But in 2012 and 2013, he seemed to crack—pun intended.

A female former mayoral candidate said Ford propositioned her and then "grabbed my ass."[3] Ex-staffers said Ford had a prostitute in the mayor's office.[4] He allegedly told a female staffer, "I banged your pussy," while drunk at a St. Patrick's Day party. Reports suggested that at the same party, Ford had knocked over a junior staffer, smashed his cell phone, and hurled racial slurs at a cabdriver.[5] Ford denied the staffer's accusation: "She says I wanted to eat her pussy, I've never said that in my life to her, I would never do that. I'm happily married, I've got more than enough to eat at home."[6] After video surfaced of Ford smoking a crack pipe—as well as video of him cryptically raging about an unknown person, "I need fucking 10 minutes to make sure he's dead"[7]—Mayor Ford was stripped by the city council of most of his powers.

Here's what's most interesting about Mayor Ford, who has steadfastly refused to resign his office. For most of his career, he was viewed as leaning to the right. (He is a registered independent.) This was largely because he was elected on a platform of cutting government waste. But as soon as Ford got into trouble with drugs, alcohol, and women, he devised a way to try to get out of the mess and hold on to his job: he proclaimed himself a liberal. He also announced he was "the best father around"—but we all know that title belongs to his role model Bill Clinton.

That's not all Clinton and Ford supposedly have in common. The mayor's brother, Doug, told the press that his brother was "a massive social liberal" who "loves" President Obama. In a move right out of the Clinton playbook, the disgraced mayor toured a housing project to promise all sorts of government handouts—a place where, according to news reports, the liberal sexual assaulter and druggie was greeted like a "rock star." He thinks he can be prime minister one day—I guess, figuring that if Clinton could paw women and get elected to America's highest office, it can work in Canada, too. So long as he's on the political left, that is.

It's an affront to the principles of liberalism, misguided though they are, that Ford thinks being a liberal will get the media to cover up for him and voters to absolve him of his sins. But here's what's more pathetic—that tactic usually works. As noted, it's worked for Bill Clinton and a whole horror show of other men who have pawed, assaulted, and otherwise abused women and gotten away with it. We could call them "Clinton's heirs."

The political arena has more than its fair share of creeps to make up for every other industry in the country, and the Democratic Party pulls much of the weight.

Just a few short months after President Obama sailed back into the White House with a victory credited to his war-on-women approach, Democrats within his party reminded the country, and women everywhere, that they had been duped about how "pro-women" the Democratic Party really is.

In July 2013, just eight months into his job as mayor, news reports started to surface about seventy-year-old Democratic mayor of San Diego Bob Filner. Filner had been a longtime ally of the Democratic Party. He was entrenched not only in California politics, but in national politics as well.

Before becoming mayor of San Diego, Filner served in Congress for twenty years representing California's Fifty-first District. Filner wasn't just any congressman from California; he was part of the powerful machine on Capitol Hill and called former House Speaker Nancy Pelosi a close friend. In fact, they founded the Congressional Progressive Caucus together.[8]

When Filner was running to be mayor of San Diego in 2012, former president Bill Clinton gave him an endorsement, going so far as to record an automated telephone call to voters. In the call, Clinton said:

> Hello, this is President Bill Clinton. I'm asking you to join me
> in supporting Bob Filner for mayor. As president I worked with

Bob to save San Diego taxpayers more than $3 billion and to secure funding for construction of a veterans' home. Bob has the experience to move San Diego forward, to create good paying twenty-first-century jobs, support quality public education, and put neighborhoods first, not special interests. As a freedom rider in the 1960s Bob showed he had the courage to do what's right. That's what he did in Congress, and that's exactly what he'll do as mayor of San Diego. Thank you.

We can now guess why Clinton saw Filner as a kindred spirit. In early July 2013, Filner was accused of sexually harassing multiple city employees, prompting his fiancée, Bronwyn Ingram, to quickly call off their engagement. After Filner initially stated there "weren't allegations to respond to,"[9] he took a page out of the Bill Clinton playbook with a maudlin, lip-biting, "I have sinned" video confession, admitting he had done something wrong without going into details:

I begin today by apologizing to you. I have diminished the office to which you elected me. The charges made at today's news conference are serious. When a friend like Donna Frye is compelled to call for my resignation, I'm clearly doing something wrong. I have reached into my heart and soul and realized I must and will change my behavior. As someone who has spent a lifetime fighting for equality for all people, I am embarrassed to admit that I have failed to fully respect the women who work for me and with me, and that at times I have intimidated them. It's a good thing that behavior that would have been tolerated in the past is being called out in this generation for what it is: inappropriate and wrong. I am also humbled to admit that I need help. I have begun to work with professionals to make changes in my behavior and approach. In addition, my staff and I will participate in sexual harassment training provided by the city.

Please know that I fully understand that only I am the one that can make these changes. If my behavior doesn't change, I cannot succeed in leading our city. In the next few days, I will be reaching out to those who now work in the Mayor's Office or have previously worked for me—both men and women—to personally apologize for my behavior. I will also be announcing fundamental changes within the Mayor's Office designed to promote a new spirit of cooperation, respect and effectiveness.

You have every right to be disappointed in me. I only ask that you give me an opportunity to prove I am capable of change, so that the vision I have for our city's future can be realized.

Filner's old pal and women's rights crusader Nancy Pelosi refused to call for Filner's resignation and said basically that what was happening in San Diego should stay in San Diego. "What goes on in San Diego is up to the people of San Diego. I'm not here to make any judgments," Pelosi said. So says the same woman who called Rush Limbaugh's comments about Sandra Fluke "obnoxious" and said Republicans were "tattooed" with the comments.[10]

So what conduct exactly was Pelosi not judging? Things got so bad, the sheriff set up a Bob Filner Abuse Hotline for people to call with tips. CNN compiled a list of some of the allegations, including not just sexual harassment but sexual assault, from more than a dozen women:

- Sixty-seven-year-old great-grandmother Peggy Shannon came forward to allege Filner repeatedly came on to her during working hours.

- Attorney Kathryn Vaughn felt Filner "making inappropriate movement" on her body after her husband left the room.
- Filner placed his hands on the behind of businesswoman Diane York after a photo.
- Real estate agent Caryl Iseman said she attended a fundraiser twenty-five years ago where Filner "decided he could reach around and grab my breast."
- Irene McCormack Jackson, Filner's former spokesperson and the first woman to go public with allegations and a lawsuit, said the mayor demanded she work without her panties on. McCormack also revealed Filner thought of women as "sexual objects or stupid idiots."
- In 2005, Filner groped the behind of consultant Laura Fink. At the time, she was the deputy manager for his congressional campaign.
- Filner made San Diego Port Tenants Association president Sharon Bernie-Cloward so uncomfortable one night after touching her inappropriately that she had someone walk her to her car after an event.
- Businesswoman Patti Roscoe went on record saying Filner put her in a headlock and tried to kiss her on numerous occasions.
- Director of government and military education at San Diego City College Lisa Curtin was licked on the cheek by Filner after he tried to kiss her and she turned away.

Possibly the worst and most disgusting move of all was when Filner exploited his power over military sexual assault victims. During his time as a congressman, the scumbag sexually harassed at least eight female veterans during his time as chairman of the House Veterans'

Affairs Committee. Women from the National Women's Veterans Association of America accused Filner of using his power as committee chairman to "access military sexual assault survivors, who they say were less likely to complain."

The group's president, Tara Jones, said Filner "went to dinners, asked women out to dinners, grabbed breasts, buttocks. The full gamut. Everything that is a complete violation of what we stand for." With good reason, Jones called Filner "a sexual predator."

To add hypocrisy to injury, while Filner was abusing his power and abusing women behind the scenes, he was publicly calling for zero-tolerance policies on sexual assault and harassment in the military. He also told nurse Michelle Tyler, who approached him asking for help for wounded veterans, that he would offer to help a brain-damaged female marine, Kathryn Raggazino, get help from Veteran's Affairs only if Tyler would have dinner with him.

"It was extremely disturbing to me that he made it very clear that his expectation was that his help for Kathryn depended on my willingness to go to dinner with him, spend personal time with him and be seen in public with him," Tyler said during a press conference. "I felt that his rubbing my arm and telling me help for Kathryn was contingent on my going out with him was extremely inappropriate and unacceptable."

At the same press conference, the marine in question, Kathryn Raggazino, said, "I don't appreciate being used as a bargaining chip to fulfill his sexual desires."

As time went on, woman after woman began to come forward with serious allegations against the mayor dubbed Filthy Filner and a serial spanker. Filner of course described himself as "a hugger" who liked to get cozy with "men and women." He entered sex rehab at the beginning of August and then after being "cured," he left early and continued "therapy" sessions on an outpatient basis.

During the course of Filner's denial of the accusations, things eventually became so creepy that female reporters were told they shouldn't be in a room alone with him, and it was strongly recommended they bring an escort with them during interviews.

After nearly two weeks of skeevy details, heavy feminist hitters in the national Democratic Party *finally* started to ask for Filner's resignation. California senator Barbara Boxer demanded Filner resign, and even Nancy "I'm-not-here-to-make-any-judgments" Pelosi got on board.

The problem is that Filner's depraved behavior had been going on for a decade before finally blowing up in 2013. It was covered up by the Democratic Party and by the liberal media, both in San Diego and in Washington, D.C.[11] "I actually had dinner over the weekend with some female members [of Congress] and former members who said that this guy has kind of been this way all along. That everybody thought that he was a little creepy, even in Washington," longtime Democratic Party insider Hilary Rosen said on CNN's *The Lead*. Pelosi and her ilk only asked for Filner's resignation after years of ignoring gross and inappropriate behavior and after public pressure for them to say something about Filner's filthy behavior.

Veteran reporter Doug Curlee detailed this failure in an op-ed:

> They are questions that should have been asked long ago, and should have been asked by those whose job it is to ask such questions: us.
>
> Who are "us"?
>
> "Us" are the San Diego news media reporters, editors, pro-

ducers and writers who pretty much knew who and what Bob Filner is and has been.

Yes, I'm including myself in that group. I've covered Bob Filner off and on since he was elected to the San Diego Unified School District Board in 1979. From the beginning, most of us saw how arrogant Filner was and is, how abusive he could be to his own staff members, how he felt elective office entitled him to be all those things and more.

We all saw that in Filner, and yet we did nothing about it. Filner was often a topic of conversation among us when we gathered at news conferences or when we would gather at the various watering holes many of us frequented together when off work.

The near universal opinion among us was, "Can you believe this guy? Why does he get away with acting like that?" Then another round of drinks would appear, and talk went on to other things.

Finally, Filner resigned after attempting to work out a major pension and benefits deal and getting his legal bills covered by San Diego taxpayers. Two months later in California state superior court, Filner pleaded guilty to felony false imprisonment and misdemeanor counts of battery against three women.

Around the same time Filner's dirty laundry began to air out, former congressman Anthony Weiner shot himself back into the spotlight. Weiner had resigned from Congress in 2011 after the public learned he had been sending sexually explicit Twitter messages to young women across the country. Although Weiner was eventually asked to resign his position in Congress by Nancy Pelosi and Debbie Wasserman Schultz, those calls didn't come until it was revealed he had been communicating with an underage Delaware girl. They kept their mouths shut regarding Weiner's treatment of his pregnant wife and the young women Weiner had been preying on in unsolicited fashion.

Then, in 2013, the public learned that, even after resigning in shame from Congress, the married father continued sexting to women half his age under the name "Carlos Danger." Pathetically, Weiner's wife, Huma Abedin, took a page out of the Clinton playbook and stood by her man in humiliation for a second time, which prompted media liberals like MSNBC's Mika Brzezinski and Andrea Mitchell to uphold her "bravery."

"Initial feelings watching this," Brzezinski tweeted, "I feel for Anthony's wife Huma. Life and love is so complicated. I think she was brave. Thoughts?" The MSNBC host added, "She looked to be in terrible pain. Again, brave. Tough."

"Brave and completely committed to him," Mitchell replied. "If he gets to a runoff it is thanks to Huma's 1st news conference appearance."

For the record, Abedin didn't look as if she was in pain. As Mitchell noted, Abedin's so-called commitment to Weiner was actually a commitment her husband's political race for mayor and her political future. She turned herself into a doormat in the name of political power, just as Hillary Clinton had done on *60 Minutes* two decades ago.

Abedin wasn't the only liberal woman who stood by Weiner. When the new scandal erupted, DNC chairwoman Debbie Wasserman Schultz said Weiner's decision to stay in the race was "a decision for Anthony Weiner to make." And Weiner campaign communications director Barbara Morgan went to extreme lengths to defend Weiner.

When Morgan learned that a former college intern named Olivia

Nuzzi had written a tell-all about the campaign in the *New York Daily News*, Morgan replied, "Fucking slutbag. Nice fucking glamour shot on the cover of the *Daily News*. Man, see if you ever get a job in this town again." In an interview with *Talking Points Memo*, Morgan added, "I mean, it's such bullshit. She could fucking, fucking twat.... You know what? Fuck you, you little cunt."

Morgan's rant didn't bother most women's groups, which, with the exception of UltraViolet, didn't bother to go out of their way to comment. But at least her foul attack on Nuzzi did not prove prescient. In the end, it was Weiner, not Nuzzi, who couldn't get a job in New York City.

While Anthony Weiner was rapidly losing popularity in the mayoral race, serial prostitute patron Eliot Spitzer was running for NYC comptroller. Spitzer, who during his time as a Democratic governor signed a law cracking down on people who did the exact same things he did, never faced a day in jail. His patronizing of prostitutes as "Client 9" was highly illegal under a law he signed making paying for sex a felony. Kristin Davis, however, the madam providing him with prostitutes, did hard time in one of the country's roughest prisons, Riker's Island.

"I spent five months at Riker's Island from which I returned penniless, homeless, and forced to take sex offender classes for five months with pedophiles and perverts while he returned to his wife in his Fifth Avenue high-rise without ever being fingerprinted, mug shot, remanded or charged with a crime under the very law he signed," Davis told the *New York Daily News*.

The Democratic Party, NOW, and other women's groups failed to come to Davis's defense and said nothing about equal treatment for men and women under the law. In fact, the pro-abortion women's group EMILY's List used the opportunity to slam Republicans and continue to uphold Democrats.

"The difference is that Republicans' words and personal actions," said EMILY's List communications director Jess McIntos, "are backed up by an actual party legislative agenda that hurts women—this stuff goes from infuriating and outrageous to genuinely frightening when they're trying to back it up with real live laws that roll back the clock to a time when women were treated as second-class citizens." McIntos added, "Republicans gaffing all over the place when it comes to women are not outliers. They are reflective of their party's actual agenda."

McIntos is the one who is not an outlier. Like so many liberal women, she allows liberal men to sexually harass women so long as they don't push legislation she disagrees with. And like so many liberal women, she makes it possible, through her silence or affirmative defense of the indefensible, for deplorable behavior to keep right on going.

Unfortunately, the examples of hypocrisy are legion. Consider several instances of men behaving badly, and ask yourself what would have happened if they had been Republicans:

SHELDON SILVER, DEMOCRAT, NEW YORK CITY— "NEW YORK'S REPUTATION AS THE LEADER ON WOMEN'S RIGHTS"

Records were released in August 2012 that New York State Assembly Speaker Sheldon Silver, often called the most powerful Democrat in the city, had authorized a secret payment of $103,080 to settle sexual harassment claims against Democratic assemblyman Vito

Lopez. Declining to discuss why he kept previous allegations from the public and used public money in a settlement, Silver was only adding to his list of slow responses to accusations of sexual misconduct while serving as the state party's most powerful state legislator for fifteen years.

In 2003, one of Silver's top aides, J. Michael Boxley, was accused of rape and later pleaded guilty to sexual misconduct. Democratic Assembly members were also involved in sex scandals with interns in 2006, 2007, and 2008. But none of these scandals were enough to merit a response from Democratic governor Andrew Cuomo, even as he rolled out his ten-point plan to "restore New York's reputation as the leader on women's rights." In fact, only two out of 107 Democratic assemblymen called for Silver to resign.

DICK HARPOOTLIAN (D-S.C.)— "YOU ARE WHAT YOU'RE NAMED"

South Carolina Democratic chairman Dick Harpootlian seems to prefer that women—particularly his governor, Nikki Haley—stick with jobs out of the political spotlight. Harpootlian made a big splash when he commented that Governor Haley should go back to "working in a dress store." When accused of rank sexism, Harpootlian said he was only suggesting that "she needs to go back to being an accountant in a dress store rather than being this fraud of a governor that we have." He also called Governor Haley "the gubernatorial equivalent of the *Real Housewives of New Jersey*," and told Democratic donors to send the Indian-American Haley "back to wherever the hell she came from." It was only after this final comment that Harpootlian was finally required to resign.

DAVID WU (D-ORE.)—"LIONS, AND TIGERS, AND BEARS, OH, MY!"

In July 2011, embattled Democratic congressman David Wu resigned amid allegations from a young woman who says he had forced an "unwanted sexual encounter" upon her. That girl was the daughter of one of Wu's friends and big campaign donors. She had recently graduated from high school.

In early 2011, the woman called Wu's office to report the incident. Wu immediately responded by saying the contact was consensual. The young woman's name was never released due to local Oregon newspaper policies protecting the names of sexual assault victims. During his college days in the 1970s, Wu reportedly got in trouble for what may have been an attempted assault, which resulted in a fight leaving Wu with scratches on his face and neck as the woman tried to get away after being smothered with a pillow for screaming. Wu claimed that his conduct was inexcusable but there was no assault and that the sexual conduct was consensual. In case you're wondering, Wu is the same guy who dressed up in a tiger costume.

MAYOR MICHAEL BLOOMBERG (I-N.Y.)— "NEW YORK'S FINEST"

As mayor of the Big Apple, Bloomberg can be said to have had quite the New York "attitude." But a New York attitude doesn't excuse someone from a long history of sexist remarks and sexual harassment. In 1996, four women filed sexual harassment suits against Bloomberg. One of the women claims that when she was pregnant,

Bloomberg told her to "kill it." He reportedly went on to lament how she was the sixteenth woman in the company to go on maternity leave.

Bloomberg, who dropped his Republican Party registration while mayor, also reportedly admitted saying, "I'd do her," but claimed later that by "do" he meant he would have a personal relationship with someone. Reports from the deposition say that Bloomberg almost stormed out of the proceedings when the opposing attorney asked him if he thought the porn film *Debbie Does Dallas* meant, "Debbie has a personal relationship with everyone from Dallas." At the same time as Bloomberg criticized Mitt Romney's social "conservatism" and endorsed Obama, he was caught telling a reporter at a holiday party to "look at the ass on her."

FORMER SENATOR CHRIS DODD (D-CONN.)— HOT TUB SLIME MACHINE

In 1985 a young woman named Carrie Fisher—yes, *that* Carrie Fisher—had dinner with Connecticut senator Chris Dodd at a swanky Washington, D.C., restaurant. Fisher wouldn't be dining alone with Dodd; fellow Beltway creep Ted Kennedy was there as well.

"Suddenly, Senator Kennedy, seated directly across from me, looked at me with his alert, aristocratic eyes and asked me a most surprising question," said Fisher.

"So," said Kennedy, "do you think you'll be having sex with Chris at the end of your date?" Dodd flashed a wide grin on a flushed face.[12]

When Fisher said no, Kennedy kept pressing and asked her if she'd be willing to have sex with Dodd in a hot tub. She again declined and said she was "no good in water." Kennedy's history with water was, of course, far from stellar.

JOHN ARNOLD (D-KY.)—"HARMLESS"

In 2013, two statehouse employees in Kentucky filed a formal complaint accusing Democratic state representative John Arnold of sexually harassing and assaulting them. One of the employees was an aide to the Democratic House majority leader. She says Arnold hit her on the butt when she bent over to pick up some bottled water. The other woman was an aide to the Democratic House majority whip. According to her, Arnold grabbed her underwear while they were walking up a flight of steps. Both women told their bosses about Arnold's harassment, but the Democratic leaders were worried that taking action against Arnold would risk their House majority, in part because Arnold's seat was not safe. They would rather protect their political party than protect women and enforce anti-discrimination laws. One of Arnold's victims said, "I feel like the people that I put my trust in to provide me a safe work environment have let me down and they continue to let me down."[13]

REP. MEL REYNOLDS (D-ILL.)—"NOBODY'S PERFECT"

Democratic congressman Mel Reynolds caught a break in 2001. His Democratic friend, outgoing president Bill Clinton, decided to commute his sentence—probably out of a feeling of mutual pity. Reynolds had been serving time for not one but two charges. After being indicted for child pornography and having sex with a sixteen-year-old girl and then attempting to cover it up, Reynolds was hit with bank fraud and campaign finance fraud while still in prison—until President Clinton handed him a get-out-of-jail-free card.

Then again, as Reynolds himself says, "Nobody's perfect." Ready to represent the Democratic Party once again, Reynolds challenged

Jesse Jackson Jr. in the 2004 race. He decided to give it another shot in 2012, joining Gus Savage—the disgraced Democratic congressman whose reputation was ruined by allegations that he had forced himself on a female Peace Corps worker in Zaire—in the race for Jesse Jackson Jr.'s seat.

To be sure, the Democrats don't have a monopoly on creepy sexists. The difference between the Democratic Party and the Republican Party, however, is that Republicans don't defend their versions of Anthony Weiner and Bob Filner. Republicans don't excuse sexist behavior just because they like the creeps' public policies. They don't say that "nobody's perfect" or that harassment is "harmless" or that "what goes on in San Diego is up to the people of San Diego; I'm not here to make any judgments."

CHAPTER 7

HOW HILLARY CLINTON BROKE THE WOMEN'S MOVEMENT

These women are trash. Nobody's going to believe them.

—Hillary Clinton

The question is, we face a lot of dangers in the world and, in the gentleman's words, we face a lot of evil men. And what in my background equips me to deal with evil and bad men?

—Hillary Clinton

As a woman and a "member of good standing" of the National Organization for Women, I stand ashamed of Hillary Clinton.

She is America's most famous enabler of abusive powerful men and, as a result, the great betrayer of everything Susan B. Anthony and every other women's rights pioneer once stood for. That's why it is galling to so many American women that Mrs. Clinton has the nerve to rest her presidential campaigns on breaking the glass ceiling. For most of her life she's lived in a glass house (actually mansion), financed by her husband's unethical conduct and shamelessness.

Hillary is the woman who looked the other way. Because she looked the other way, her husband was allowed to demean and humiliate scores of women. Because she looked the other way, Bill Clinton's behavior became a template for impressionable boys and young men for whom mauling interns and cheating on your wife is socially acceptable "private behavior." Because she looked the other way, the women's movement has become a partisan joke. And of course because she looked the other way, Hillary Clinton became a successful politician as a quid pro quo. It's well known that she was a hated, divisive political figure—considered a liar by people on the left and the right—until her husband's cheating with Monica Lewinsky made everyone feel sorry for her. That's the only reason she had any chance of winning a Senate seat in New York.

Think about that—Hillary Clinton allowed a young girl to be lied about, manipulated, and persecuted so that she and her loathsome husband could hold on to power. I ask American women who grow teary-eyed at the thought of Hillary Clinton breaking the "glass ceiling": What is so admirable about any of that?

Her behavior is not only disgusting. It is heartbreaking. It is sad.

It is also decades old. "The one who I really hold responsible as the enabler is Hillary because Hillary knew about our relationship three months into it," Gennifer Flowers told me. "She had no intentions of doing anything about it because she wasn't about to let anything disturb her power structure that she was building and get in the way of her goals. She sacrificed women as well."

It wasn't just the Gennifer Flowers affair Hillary tolerated. It was an entire list of women coming forward with sexual allegations against her husband. Naturally, instead of holding Bill accountable for his actions, she shifted blame somewhere else. Every time her husband was accused of sexual misconduct, Hillary and the Clintons' minions attempted to defame the accusers as liars, crazies, gold diggers, stalkers, and sluts.

"The great story here for anybody willing to find it and write about it and explain it is this vast right-wing conspiracy that has been conspiring against my husband since the day he announced for president," Hillary Clinton said in response to the Monica Lewinsky scandal, which of course Bill Clinton flat-out denied with the famous statement, "I did not have sexual relations with that woman."

These days, the Clinton PR operation is taking a moment or two away from demonizing Bill's many female accusers so they can rewrite the history of her do-nothing State Department as some big moment for the advancement of women. When the women's group EMILY's List recounted her greatest moments as secretary of state, they quoted at length from Clinton's speech at the Women in the World Summit.[1] But Secretary Clinton wasn't helping women around the world. She was covering up for abusers once again, this time in the State Department.

In June 2013, CBS News reported the details of a State Department memo revealing rampant cover-ups, scandals, and sexual misconduct from senior officials, including a U.S. ambassador. The memo showed many investigations were ignored, brushed under the rug, excused, and interfered with in order to cover up and stave off embarrassment.

In one case, a State Department security official stationed in Beirut was accused of engaging in multiple sexual assaults. Many members of Clinton's security detail were accused of regularly hiring young female prostitutes during official State Department trips in countries around the world. A U.S. ambassador was accused of routinely ditching "his protective security detail in order to solicit sexual favors from both prostitutes and minor children" in a nearby park.[2] In 2013, a U.S. Embassy official was removed for allegedly trading visas for sexual favors. The *New York Post* reported female State Department whistleblower Kerry Howard was "run out of the foreign service," lost her job, and was "bullied" after revealing that U.S. Consul General Donald Moore engaged in sexual activities with women inside his office and with call girls in Naples.[3] Moore allegedly pressured one mistress who worked for him to get an abortion and have her tubes tied.[4]

"It's cover-up after cover-up. It's absolutely hideous," Howard told the *Post*. "When our diplomats disrespect the Italians by hiring and firing them because they have seen too much—or use them for 'sex-ercise'—we have to question why we have diplomats abroad at taxpayer expense."

Watchdogs whose job it is to keep the State Department accountable were reportedly told to stand down and back off when it came to following up on potential cases of sexual assault and drug abuse. One of those watchdogs, former State Department inspector general Aurelia Fedenisn, provided CBS News with information about the ongoing obstruction of investigations and described an "intimidation campaign" against her. Fedenisn's attorney told *The Cable*, "They had law enforcement officers camp out in front of her house, harass her children and attempt to incriminate herself."[5]

When State Department spokesperson and former Obama for America traveling press secretary Jen Psaki was asked about the allegations, she promised the country that department employees are held to the "highest standards," and that they take "allegations of misconduct seriously and we investigate thoroughly."

Psaki also pushed back on the idea that the department was neither interested in accountability nor guilty of a cover-up. "The notion that we would not vigorously pursue criminal misconduct in a case, any case, is preposterous," she said during a press conference, adding emphasis that this type of misconduct was in no way "endemic" within the department. But Psaki either was not informed about the numerous cases within the State Department or she was lying.

State Department officials (and the Obama administration in general) are constantly citing "ongoing criminal investigations within a department" as a reason they can't comment on or take responsibility for a situation. It turns out, at least in the State Department, the so-called internal investigation was being sidelined by people within the department.

When she left her post as secretary of state in early 2013, Hillary Clinton left allegations of sexual assault and cases of sex trafficking of minors wide open with zero consequences. Her security team was left unscathed and staffers were promoted.

While the lives of whistleblowers have been destroyed and changed forever,[6] the men they exposed are living quite nicely. An ambassador was given a "retire early" card without prosecution arising from allegations of having sex with prostitutes overseas. A consul general is now teaching at a war college and still receiving a State Department paycheck. A former security officer who was named in the bombshell IG memo and accused of sexual assault now occupies a swanky office as a special agent in a diplomatic department in Washington, D.C.

Clinton was willing to cover up for those engaged in misconduct for political purposes and for her own personal political gain. Ambassador Gutman raised five hundred thousand dollars for Barack Obama's presidential campaign before joining the State Department and allegedly soliciting prostitutes and minors. If Clinton were to hold her security detail accountable, they could potentially derail a 2016 campaign for the White House through dirt of their own on her.

Covering up the sex crimes of the State Department also allows President Obama to get away with delivering high-minded speeches about the horrors of international sex crimes. "It ought to concern every person, because it is a debasement of our common humanity," Obama said. "It ought to concern every community, because it tears at our social fabric. It ought to concern every business, because it distorts markets. It ought to concern every nation, because it endangers public health and fuels violence and organized crime. I'm talking about the injustice, the outrage, of human trafficking, which must be called by its true name—modern slavery."

The women's movement has had little to say about these outrageous abuses within the Obama administration. And for obvious reasons. The movement has become a partisan shill covering for Democrat misbehavior.

I hold Hillary Clinton responsible for what's become of the women's movement. Because Hillary has been its role model, she's turned the women's movement into a pathetic joke. They have lost any moral authority or credibility. Instead, they have become nothing more than public-relations operations for Democratic politicians, so long as those politicians support twenty-four-hour abortions.

As StopPatriarchy.org, a NOW-affiliated organization, put it, women deserve the right to an abortion "on demand and without apology."[7] Oh, and also vagina napkins. Let's not forget those.

Here's a sampling of the women's rights movement and its priorities today.

VAGINA NAPKINS FOR ABORTION

To further their grand goals, always classy NARAL activists auction off napkins rubbed on the lady parts of pro-abortion female celebrities to raise money for abortions.

"@SarahKSilverman is auctioning a napkin she's rubbed on her vagina—donate at #vagnapkin. Not kidding. Kinda want it. #TEXASWOMENFOREVER," NARAL board member and self-described feminist author Jessica Valenti tweeted on November 18, 2013.

When I tweeted that the vagina napkin fiasco was part of why I'm glad I'm not part of the feminist movement and that Valenti's timeline was making me nauseated, she responded by telling me, "That's okay, we don't want you."

Fund Texas Women, an organization that provides information to women seeking abortions, followed up with their own tweet, writing, "Tweet with the hashtag #VAGNAPKIN if you want to bid on something AWESOME from Sarah Silverman! #texaswomenforever."

Sarah Silverman, a self-proclaimed "comedian," described the napkin move as "feministing." She has a long history of promoting abortion and even did a video for Comedy Central showing her "looking back on her three abortions" and shows a disappointed Silverman when she finds out she can't have any more. In the background, Green Day's "Time of Your Life" plays.

DEBATING THE BEST AGE FOR ABORTIONS

The feminist blog *Jezebel* never fails to disappoint with vulgarity from its writers, but in February 2013, news editor Erin Gloria Ryan managed to go the extra mile to prove the site hadn't hit the moral bottom yet. In a piece titled "What's the Best Age to Have an Abortion," Ryan took the time to break down each age bracket at which a woman might find herself pregnant. A graphic of tree rings and "time to abort" was used to demonstrate when women should have an abortion.

For women under 18, Ryan describes the option of abortion as, "Well, duh. This one's a no brainer." To women 18 to 23, she suggests abortion, but laments young women still on their parents' health insurance may not be able to hide it from their folks. To women ages 24 to 27, she states, "As a rule, it's more emotional to abort when you know the guy's last name," and that settling down with that "one special guy" instead of sleeping around might make it possible not to want to abort. Inching into the thirties, Ryan suggests women from 30 to 34 have kids if they want them because once 35 to 40 rolls around, abortion is necessary to get rid of the babies with birth defects in order to make life more convenient. Ultimately Ryan concluded the best time for women to have an abortion is at age 25. I guess that's something for you women to look forward to.

BIRTH CONTROL FOR GRANNIES

In 2013 the White House promoted Obamacare by reminding women under sixty-five that they can get free birth control under the new health-care law.

"Thanks to the #ACA, 1 in 3 women under 65 gained access to preventative care—like birth control—with no out of pocket costs. #HappyMothersDay," a tweet from the official White House Twitter feed said.

This was a strange statement, especially considering the reason it was issued—to celebrate Mother's Day.

BIG DECISIONS: JOGGING? OR ABORTION?

To mark the fortieth anniversary of *Roe v. Wade*, NARAL, one of the largest pro-abortion groups in the country, produced a video called *Choice Out Loud*. The video was made with a goal of showing the world that "every decision has a story" and depicts forty women making simple decisions such as going for a jog, swimming, showering, and brushing their hair, implying that these are choices equal to the choice to have an abortion.

VOTE WITH YOUR LADY PARTS

On October 2, 2012, someone thought it would a good idea to reach out to women through the official BarackObama.com Tumblr website. How? By posting an e-card showing a woman and the text, "Vote like your lady parts depend on it," with the subtext commentary, "Because they kinda do."

The message from Team Obama was clear: Don't vote with your brain, ladies, vote with your genitals. It was also a clear picture of how Democrats saw women as voters.

After massive backlash on social media, the image was eventually deleted, but the "voting with lady parts" theme continued in less explicit detail until the end of the election cycle and beyond.

In March 2013, *Sex and the City* star Sarah Jessica Parker stated Hillary Clinton would make a good president in 2016 because "the conventionally female parts of her can partner well with the parts of her that are considered not as female to make a great leader."

THE VAGINA MONOLOGUES

The Vagina Monologues is a play written by Eve Ensler, first produced in 1996. It has been published in forty-five languages and performed in more than 120 countries and shows women openly talking about their body parts and engaging in sexual re-enactments on stage for everyone to see. Throughout the course of the play we see different scenarios played out.

One scene shows a tax attorney who leaves her profession to become a sex worker. According to the play, she "loves to please women." This scene shows the former attorney talking about how boring tax law is in comparison to her new occupation, implying that oral sex in a paying stranger's bedroom is a more rewarding career path than oral arguments in a courtroom. Another scene details the experience of a woman who attends an orgasm workshop, which requires participation in group masturbation. The actress in this scene says her private parts are "the essence of me, both the doorbell to my house and the house itself," implying those parts are what make up the essence of a woman, which is exactly the opposite of what pre-1960s women's rights activists wanted. The entire purpose of the original women's rights movement was to get society to see women as human beings equal to men through their successes and hard work, not through their body parts. At one point, the audience is asked to participate by chanting, "C*nt! C*nt! C*nt!" over and over again. The play endorses child rape—it calls a thirteen-year-old's drunken sexual encounter with an older woman "a good rape"—and men are portrayed only as rapists and cheating abusers, never as human beings who can be partners in life. The details get even more graphic, but I'll spare you.

The claim by Ensler and her supporters is that the play empowers women and raises awareness about violence against women as it travels to different countries around the world. Sure, money raised from the play is sent to communities that use it in some ways to help victims of violence, but the play frustrates a (relatively modest) goal of the original women's rights movement: to eliminate the notion that women are defined by their sex organs.

NOW: BOWLING FOR ABORTION

Sometimes during emotional debates about abortion, in order to come off as compassionate and concerned, NOW activists will make the argument that the choice to have an abortion is a "very tough choice to make" for many women. But looking at the way NOW activists celebrate abortion tells a very different story about how they really feel about the issue.

Take for example the National Abortion Access Bowl-a-Thon held each year in April, which is described by NOW this way on the official website: "The Bowl-a-Thon is a nationwide series of local events that allow community members (you!) to captain your own bowling team, participate in a kickass national event—and raise money to help women and girls pay for abortions they couldn't otherwise afford. Abortion funds are local, grassroots groups that work tirelessly to help low-income disadvantaged women who want an abortion and do not have enough money to pay for it."

You read that correctly, to "help women and *girls* pay for abortions."

The slogan for the event is, "We're going balls out for abortion funding." Participants are encouraged to choose a "brilliant and punny team name." Those "punny" team names include Misoproselytizers, Ova Achievers, Texas' Puck Ferrys, and New Orleans' Preaux

Choice. The hashtag #bowl13 is used on Twitter so people can share their bowling for abortion stories. NOW also set ups a Flickr account each year featuring smiling participants in costumes, heart signs, and T-shirts that say "rolling overy" or bright orange "clinic escort" vests. Bowling pins are also set up with photos of people like Texas senator Ted Cruz, Texas governor Rick Perry, and other pro-life politicians.

The event, as stated in the slogan, is used as a fundraiser in order to give women and *girls* money to have abortions, raking in more than $1 million since it was started five years ago. The money is collected nationwide through a series of bowl-a-thon events in different cities, equal to the cost of approximately three thousand abortions.

To be a feminist hero in the new feminist movement there are a few main things you must accomplish, all of which include vulgarity and degradation.

HOSURANCE

On November 12, 2013, a group out of Colorado known as Progress-Now produced a series of misogynist and degrading advertisements promoting Obamacare. The ad campaign, hosted on DoYouGot Insurance.com, portrayed young people as sex-crazed, drunken losers who only care about getting laid and partying. The way the ads portrayed young women was even worse. The mastermind behind the ads, naturally, was bro-choicer Alan Franklin. He serves as the political director for ProgressNow Colorado.

"Hey girl, you're excited about easy access to birth control and I'm excited about getting to know you. She got insurance. Now you can too. Thanks Obamacare!" said one ad featuring a young blond woman in a black dress openly holding a package of birth control pills next to a cutout of actor Ryan Gosling.

"Let's get physical. OMG, he's hot! Let's hope he's as easy to get as this birth control. My health insurance covers the pill, which means all I have to worry about is getting him between the covers.* I got insurance. Thanks Obamacare!" another ad stated. It showed a young woman again holding a package of birth control in front of a young man with his hand on her hip. The fine print of the ad read "*The pill doesn't protect you from STDs, condoms and common sense do that."

The advertisements were so over the top, Planned Parenthood of Colorado thought they were put out by GOP operatives to attack Obamacare and to "slut shame" women.

"Unfortunate that anti-obamacare folks are #slutshaming #women who use #birthcontrol #GotInsurance #ThanksObamacare," Planned Parenthood of Colorado tweeted.

When they found out the ads were produced by ProgressNow Colorado in promotion of Obamacare, Planned Parenthood defended the ads.

Franklin never issued an apology. Instead, he argued that women who found them offensive were attacking women's rights. Franklin's defense and attempt to change the subject wasn't surprising. Another sexist liberal male who created sexist ads to degrade women and portray them as simple sex objects? We shouldn't be shocked.

As a member "in good standing," I contacted the National Organization for Women through their public relations firm Scott Circle, specifically emailing Vice President Sarah Coppersmith, since she regularly sends out NOW press releases, asking for a comment about the advertisements considering the sexist content. Coppersmith didn't respond, but a woman named Megan Vibert from the same firm did.

"Apologies for the delay in getting back but NOW was unavailable for comment yesterday on the ads," Vibert said.

I responded by asking, "Are they available to comment today?" I never received a response. This is how NOW treats its members?

GIANT VAGINA COSTUMES

In August 2012, activists from the anti-war group Code Pink descended upon the RNC convention in Tampa, Florida, to protest and fight the war on women they alleged Republicans were waging. Their goal was to get attention and they most certainly did. The outfit of choice? Massive vagina costumes. Life-sized.

I tracked down Code Pink's national coordinator Alli McCracken to ask what the point was. She said the goal of the vagina costumes was to send a message about keeping Republicans out of women's health care, and she explained the group was outraged over Democratic Michigan state representative Lisa Brown getting booted from the Michigan House floor for breaking rules about language and decorum after she said "vagina" during a debate.

The display was horrifying.

TAMPON EARRINGS

After a segment about a new late-term abortion ban in Texas, MSNBC host and self-proclaimed defender of women's rights Melissa Harris-Perry thanked her producer for hanging tampons on earring hooks, which she proceeded to then put into her ears before the break. Somehow the tampons were representing a protest of abortion and a promotion of women's rights.

"My producer Lorena made for me last week some tampon earrings. The Texas state legislature said that you couldn't bring tampons in, when these women were going to, in fact, stand up for their own reproductive rights," she said to viewers.

What Harris-Perry didn't explain is the reason why police didn't allow tampons to be openly brought into the Texas Capitol: Previously used tampons were being used by protesters to throw at pro-life lawmakers. Naturally, Harris-Perry insinuated that women were being discriminated against for their feminine sanitation needs, which was far from the case. Other items such as bricks, glitter, confetti, condoms, jars of urine, and jars of feces were also confiscated by police officers.

BRO-CHOICE MOVEMENT

The bro-choice movement, made up of men who are militantly pro-abortion in order to protect their casual sex lives, has been around for a long time. But this sector of the pro-choice movement really got attention in the summer of 2013 when the Texas legislature passed a bill, HB-2, banning abortion after five months of pregnancy. This spawned massive protests from rabid feminists, who naturally are supported by men who support abortion for the sake of skirting responsibility.

Pro-abortion activist, proud bro-choicer, and progressive Texas blogger Ben Sherman explained the phenomenon quite well in a blog post at the time titled "Bro-Choice: How #HB2 Hurts Texas Men Who Like Women."[8] It was an ode to selfishness.

"Forcing women to adhere to the anti-choice attitudes of state legislators forces men to do the same, and will have serious consequences both on men's lives and lifestyles," Sherman wrote. He added:

You want to decide when and if to have kids. This bill will force thousands of Texas men into unplanned fatherhood by making it impossible for women to access an abortion in the event of an unplanned pregnancy. Even if you want to have kids, you probably don't want an accident to make you a father before you're psychologically ready and able to care for a child. If you don't want kids, you don't want the narrow, personal views of politicians in the state government to force you to have them.

Your sex life is at stake. Can you think of anything that kills the vibe faster than a woman fearing a back-alley abortion? Making abortion essentially inaccessible in Texas will add an anxiety to sex that will drastically undercut its joys. And don't be surprised if casual sex outside of relationships becomes far more difficult to come by.

There's not much that can take a moral compass any farther south than supporting abortion in order to ensure, as a male, your casual sex life is uninhibited. What's worse? The fact that feminists support and appreciate the bro-choicers. In return for feminist support for men like Sherman, women engage in the very patriarchy they claim to be fighting against.

CHAPTER 8

BARACK OBAMA: THE MOST ANTI-WOMAN PRESIDENT EVER

I felt like a piece of meat.

—*Christina Romer, former Obama administration official*

Okay, maybe at first glance, this chapter title seems a little unfair. Is Obama worse for women than presidents in the eighteenth and nineteenth centuries, when women couldn't even vote? Worse than the sexist Woodrow Wilson, the misogynist JFK, and the serial sexual assaulter Bill Clinton?

Folks, hear me out.

For starters, Woodrow Wilson never pretended to be the president of American women. Kennedy and Clinton did not rely single-handedly on the women's vote to cling to office or craft almost all of their policies to manipulate women into thinking they were on the verge of being handcuffed to their kitchen sinks and forced to churn out baby after baby without access to birth control. That's what Barack Obama wants every woman to think. That he is the only thing stopping a Republican steamrolling of women's rights that starts with stealing their condoms and ends in a national campaign to get women out of the workforce and into the home.

I'll spell it out as plainly as I can: Obama is the worst president for women because he has systematically lied to them. He has brazenly campaigned as their champion, even as he seeks to make them wards of the state, forever dependent on government largesse in the form of food stamps and free birth control. He's claimed to work for their best interests, and yet screwed them at every opportunity. (Unlike with Kennedy and Clinton, that word is not to be taken literally.) Even Mitt Romney has figured it out. As he told me, "If there has been an administration which has been hard on women, it's this one." In the Obama worldview, women aren't human beings capable of charting their own destiny at home or the workplace just as men are, they are dependents in desperate need of government handouts and abortions.

So I say again. Barack Obama is the most anti-women president in American history. Still sounds shocking, doesn't it?

You never hear anyone say that in the media (though such things were often said about Reagan and Bush). Oprah didn't warn anybody when she cozied up to Obama in 2008 and proclaimed him the second most important person in the world (Oprah of course being number one). Democrats certainly don't think that the Obama administration has been harmful to women. And you know what? Neither do most Republicans. We've all been trained to think that Democrats are good to women and Republicans need to clean up their act, even as the last liberal hero, Mr. Obama, systematically damages the interests and futures of American women.

Now let me make the case.

INDICTMENT 1: ATMOSPHERE OF SEXISM

It's a not-so-well-kept secret in Washington that the Obama White House is a testosterone-fueled boys club, where women get short shrift. Obama's former head of the Council of Economic Advisors, Christina Romer, said of her time in the Obama White House, "I felt like a piece of meat." Obama's former White House communications director Anita Dunn told Obama aide Valerie Jarrett that the White House "actually fit all of the classic legal requirements for a genuinely hostile workplace to women."[1]

President Obama has no one to blame for that atmosphere but himself. He has gone golfing more than 150 times since taking office back in 2009. On all but a few occasions, he golfed only with men. His top eighteen golf partners are all men. He's gone through stretches of time spanning two years without playing a single round with a female in the golf cart. No female staffers, aides, or secretaries. When he does choose to golf with women, it's usually with Health and Human Services secretary Kathleen Sebelius, on whom he relies to implement Obamacare. They've gone golfing twice. (Maybe on one of those rounds she could have given him a fore! on what a disaster his signature legislative achievement was going to be.) The only other golf outing with a woman was with domestic policy advisor Melody Barnes in 2009.[2]

The *New York Times*[3] reported on the issue and said, "The technical foul over the all-male game has become a nagging concern for a White House that has battled an impression dating to the presidential campaign that Mr. Obama's closest advisers form a boys' club and that he is too frequently in the company only of men—not just when playing sports, but also when making big decisions."

Time magazine writer Amy Sullivan[4] further pointed out the problem. "There's a looseness to Obama when he's hanging out with the boys club that doesn't appear in co-ed gatherings. Sometimes he even literally engages in locker room humor," she said in an article about Obama's "woman problem." She reported, "The President blows off steam on the golf course with male colleagues and friends. He takes to the White House basketball court with NBA stars, men's college players, and male cabinet members and members of Congress."

Obama's exact response to criticism over all-male basketball games and excluding of female voices in the White House was, "I gotta say, I think this is bunk."[5] That same year, Obama was forced to hold a dinner with female aides so they could explain their concerns and complaints of being boxed out of the inner circle. A photo released of the dinner showed the women with their frustration clearly written on their faces.

"Other senior women have complained that their arguments seemed to disappear into the ether at meetings, unacknowledged by Obama," wrote *Time*'s Sullivan, noting that Obama's first communications director, Ellen Moran, left the White House after just ninety-two days. "These complaints will ring familiar to most professional women. And we know that the difference between temporary annoyances and an intolerable situation is a boss who acknowledges the issue and moves quickly to address it. Yet it seems to have taken several years for Obama to pay even minimal attention to the problem."

Obama has done little to address his lack of regard for female voices in meetings or for major decision making. On the other hand, when the Republican House of Representatives organizes basketball games, women are invited to participate.

INDICTMENT 2: EQUAL PAY FOR WOMEN

For all of his stated support of "equal pay for women" and his end-less attacks on Republicans over the issue, Obama is paying women working in his White House substantially less than men. Financial reports detailing Obama's first term show that in 2011 alone, there was an $11,000 difference between the average salaries of men and women working in the White House. Those making the top salary of $172,200 included fourteen men and just six women. The average woman working in the White House makes $60,000, while the aver-age male makes $71,000, an 18 percent difference. The majority of the people occupying the lowest-paid positions in the White House are women.

When it comes to major positions, Obama's cabinet in both his first and second terms has been full of men, and just 10 percent of his appointed "czars" are women. Obama only appointed Janet Yellen to head the Fed after Larry Summers pulled his name from the run-ning.

INDICTMENT 3: PATTERNS OF DISCRIMINATION AND SEXUAL HARASSMENT

In November 2010, Department of Justice civil rights attorney Christy McCormick filed a complaint of employment discrimina-tion. She claimed her former supervisors "subjected her to a pattern of unfavorable treatment that included persistent hostile verbal and non-verbal behaviors towards her and other women in the office; humiliation; belittlements; disrespect; intimidation; disregard; exclu-sion; character and work ethic assassination; condescension; avoidance; isolation; invasion of privacy; undercutting and undermining with regard to job assignments, and assignment of credit to other persons (males) for work performed."

McCormick voluntarily served on behalf of the Justice Department at the U.S. Embassy in Baghdad, Iraq, from October 2009 to October 2010. In September 2009, Chief Justice of Iraq Madhat Al-Mahmood visited the National Center for State Courts (NCSC) in Williamsburg, Virginia, where McCormick lives. Despite having an upcoming deployment to Iraq to work on rule of law issues, help professionalize the court system, and work on transition responsibilities from military to civilian authorities, McCormick was not told about Al-Mahmood's visit. She found out about it by visiting the NCSC website while searching for a state code of judicial ethics in Arabic for the chief justice of the Kurdish Supreme Court. As part of her assignment in Baghdad, she regularly met with Al-Mahmood to discuss judicial issues.

"I was [already] in Baghdad when I discovered that the Chief Justice visited Williamsburg the week before I deployed," McCormick told me. "That is when I wrote to Doug Allen." He was her Baghdad supervisor, who was in charge of the Iraq mission on behalf of the deputy attorney general.

"Wish I had known he was going to be in Williamsburg," wrote McCormick, "I would have tried to see him and invite him to my home."

"He would've liked your mac and cheese," Allen responded.

McCormick explained to me that "the reason why Allen mentioned mac and cheese is because I made mac and cheese for the Rule of Law office's Thanksgiving dinner, held at Allen's Embassy apartment in Iraq, which was potluck. Everyone either made something or picked something up from the dining facility to bring to the dinner. I highly doubt that Allen would have made that comment to one of the male attorneys had he said he would have invited the Chief Justice to his home—or to his house."

Once in Baghdad, she served as the DOJ elections expert in Iraq and helped oversee the March 2010 Iraq national elections, a high-risk and dangerous job. She monitored polling places and ballot collection and centers and provided regular reports from voting locations for the Embassy. She's also headed election observation efforts in jurisdictions all over the United States for the Justice Department. Her reports were used by the ambassador to brief high-level officials back in Washington about the Iraqi elections, and she briefed the deputy attorney general on the election through secured video teleconference.

Throughout her year in Iraq, McCormick was discriminated against because of her gender. Operating in a hostile work environment, she was repeatedly subjected to unfavorable treatment and hostile verbal and non-verbal behavior. Credit for her work was given to males in the office, and her efforts went unacknowledged by her supervisors. When she brought these discriminatory actions to the attention of management, McCormick was retaliated against and received retribution for daring to speak out. She was told she was "too assertive," something that would never be said to a male attorney in the same position, and was negatively compared to two male staff members whom she often supervised.

"While I was working at the Embassy, I observed persistent sexual harassment and discrimination against women," Barbara Mulvaney said in a declaration in the case. "Everything at the Embassy was geared toward males, and the men behaved as if it was a 'Boys' Club.' Women were routinely harassed, disregarded, passed over in favor of males, omitted from meetings, condescended to, and their contributions to the mission were not valued. It was not unusual for women to have to endure comments about their looks, their intellect or what they were wearing. They had to tolerate being objectified and humiliated every day. This was an accepted culture at the embassy."

The working atmosphere of the embassy was described as offensive, intimidating, and abusive by many of McCormick's colleagues.

Before going to Baghdad, McCormick had a wealth of experience under her belt. She had traveled to more than fifty different countries and had always received high evaluations from her supervisors and uniform praise from peers. When McCormick was an assistant attorney general in Virginia, she worked on two important cases to the Supreme Court, *Virginia v. Black* and *Virginia v. Hicks*. After being out of law school for only two years, McCormick was tapped to work with the Virginia solicitor general on appellate work to the Fourth Circuit Court of Appeals—and then on Supreme Court cases. In both Supreme Court cases, she worked on writing the briefs and on preparing the solicitor general for oral argument. She was admitted into the Supreme Court Bar in 2003.

While in Iraq, McCormick helped train Iraqi government officials through the office of the rule of law coordinator.

During training of female cadets for Iraqi police positions, Iraqi colonel Sabah Hoshi Mohammed, director of police training qualification, engaged her in a debate in front of the female cadets about how men are allowed to treat and "discipline" women according to the Koran. Her position was that men abusing and violently assaulting women should not be able to hide behind the Koran. Afterward, several stunned female cadets told her they never could have imagined witnessing such a debate, between a man and a woman, over the Koran. McCormick stood up for those women and encouraged

Sabah to empower women and to mentor female police cadets at the Baghdad Police Academy.

During her time in Baghdad, McCormick's efforts to build a new government went unacknowledged by supervisors, but things like her cooking and attire did not. "The two men probably yelled at everyone in the office at some point, but it seemed to me they were more sarcastic and demeaning in the way they treated women," said Jason Patil, a trial attorney for the Department of Justice. McCormick alleges that supervisor Michael Gunnison "tended to mock her first by repeating her words in a high-pitched voice, before yelling at her. . . . It seemed to me that Mr. Gunnison generally thought of women in an old-fashioned way, only really noting their cooking or appearance, and expecting them to defer to his wishes. I recall Mr. Gunnison commenting on Ms. McCormick making him chicken soup when he was sick, but I don't recall Mr. Gunnison praising her for the legitimate work she did in the office. Mr. Gunnison would sometimes comment on Ms. McCormick's choice of clothing. I recall once when she wore a black outfit; Mr. Gunnison asked if there was a funeral that day. I recall Mr. Gunnison sometimes asking her if she was really going to wear the clothing she had selected for that day. In my opinion, she always dressed professionally."

During her time in Baghdad, McCormick had to miss a day of work due to a medical issue that required attention at Sather Air Force Base, also in the Green Zone. Because it was an emergency, the Embassy's medical doctor ordered her to be transported from the Embassy to the Air Force hospital by medevac helicopter. McCormick alleged that instead of being supportive, Supervisor Robert Morean made several phone calls to the medical office and Air Force hospital in an attempt to gain private information on her medical issue, and when she returned to the office, accused McCormick of not following appropriate protocol in requesting permission for her absence in advance. When Morean was eventually approached about his treatment of women in the OROLC, he said women in the office were "lazy, incompetent, and did not have the skills they needed to do their jobs."

The Justice Department did not provide the employees it sent to Iraq with a procedure for reporting sexual harassment or gender discrimination, so the Rule of Law Office employees were on their own in figuring out how to deal with the escalating hostile atmosphere due to the supervisors' discrimination. After trying to deal with the situation on their own without success, McCormick and Patil decided to inform Allen and others in the Office of the attorney general. Gary Grindler, then acting deputy attorney general, who had oversight responsibility of the supervisors, was provided daily briefs on the hostile atmosphere in the Baghdad office. When he realized that the situation had escalated to an unacceptable level, he called the supervisors back to Washington to counsel them about their behavior. Instead of replacing them and putting a stop to the discriminatory atmosphere, he sent them back to Baghdad, where they continued their misconduct against McCormick and other women there unabated. His staff instructed the complaining employees to keep quiet about it, because of fears it would embarrass the department and put State Department funding for the Iraq program in jeopardy.

Patil eventually advised McCormick and other women in the office to consider filing an Equal Employment Opportunity (EEO) complaint in response to their sustained poor treatment. Because the Justice Department had not provided an EEO counselor in Iraq, McCormick had to use the State Department's procedures and reported the discrimination to one of its EEO counselors in Iraq. Not surprisingly, the evidence in support of the complaint was substantial. For example, Jenifer Moore, a highly regarded career foreign service officer with the State Department, declared under oath that sexual harassment and near assault were widespread at the Embassy and were ignored by supervisors.

Moore said, "In general, women were treated very poorly at Embassy Baghdad. There were few women in positions of leadership, and the atmosphere on the Embassy Compound was very unfavorable toward females. Everything was geared toward men, and women received little credit or respect for their work. Sexual harassment was rampant and consciously permitted by supervisors and leadership. Women were routinely ignored, dismissed, and patronized throughout the Embassy, and condescending comments about women's clothing, or about them having limited intellectual abilities, or about their physical appearance were often made and tolerated, including my office [INL] and in the OROLC under Mr. Allen and subsequently under Mr. Gunnison."

Unfortunately, it wasn't just verbal abuse and character assassinations that these women suffered in Baghdad. Physical harassment was a daily event. According to Moore, "Complaints were made about men grazing women's breasts and staring at them, and there was a general fear among the females for their safety on the Embassy compound and in the Green Zones. Complaints were ignored and glossed over."

When McCormick officially filed her complaint with the Office of Equal Employment Opportunity, she received further retaliation and reprisal from her supervisors and from the Deputy Attorney General's Office. Allen sabotaged McCormick by blocking her from promotions in Baghdad and by giving her negative job references and evaluations. While the ambassador in Iraq gave McCormick the Meritorious Honor Award for her extraordinary achievements there, Allen wrote a review of McCormick's work that said she merely "met expectations."

When McCormick returned to the Department of Justice in Washington, D.C., she was, along with the other Justice Department employees who served in Iraq, given an award by Deputy Attorney General James Cole. At the award ceremony, she was cited not solely for her work in rule of law or her substantive accomplishments, such as training new female police cadets, but for being the "best cook in Baghdad." As of the writing of this book, McCormick's complaint has not been fully adjudicated and her allegations have not been proven.

As the previous chapter's examination of Hillary Clinton's State Department demonstrated, Embassy Baghdad was hardly an isolated case of endemic sexism in the Obama administration.

INDICTMENT 4: USING THE IRS TO KEEP WOMEN OUT OF POLITICS

In May 2009, President Barack Obama "joked" about targeting political opponents through the IRS during a commencement speech at Arizona State University. After ASU refused to give him an honorary degree (because he was new to the job and didn't yet deserve one), Obama said, "I really thought this was much ado about nothing, but I do think we all learned an important lesson. I learned never again to pick another team over the Sun Devils in my NCAA brackets." Then came the kicker: "President [Michael] Crowe and the Board of Regents will soon learn all about being audited by the IRS."

What came after Obama's "joke" about the IRS was chilling. Just a month before his speech, Americans across the country had attended Tea (taxed enough already) Party rallies expressing their outrage over runaway government spending, bailouts, and stimulus. One year later, nearly one hundred thousand taxpayers marched on Washington and Barack Obama knew he had a problem on his hands. It wasn't long before Republicans regained the House of Representatives in a historic victory, and they introduced a new brand of fiscal conservatism that would wreak havoc on Obama's agenda.

President Obama started calling out Tea Party groups in his speeches, while Democrats like Harry Reid took to the Senate floor to lament Tea Party "extremism." Meanwhile, the IRS was paying attention. They started deliberately targeting conservative groups based on their beliefs, singling out words and phrases like "Tea Party," "9/12," "Patriot," and "Constitution." Officials told IRS workers to flag anything that seemed "anti-Obama" or "anti-government."

In March 2012, the House Oversight Committee sent an inquiry to the IRS about potential inappropriate targeting of conservative groups after constituents issued complaints to Congress saying they were receiving harassment and inappropriate questions from the agency. Lois Lerner, director of tax exempt organizations at the time, told Congress everything was fine and that groups were not being treated inappropriately.

By May 2013, Lerner was singing a different tune. She publicly apologized for the inappropriate targeting of conservative groups, hoping the whole thing would blow over before the release of a damning inspector general's report. That didn't happen. When called by Congress to testify about her involvement in the scandal, Lerner said she did nothing wrong, pleaded the Fifth Amendment, and was sent off on a three-month paid vacation before deciding to retire. When recalled back to Congress in March 2014, she pled the Fifth for a second time.

What was left out of this story is the fact that an incredible amount of Tea Party groups across the country were started by women, many of whom were getting involved in politics for the very first time: Dianne Belsom, founder of the Laurens Country Tea Party; Becky Gerritson, founder of the Wetumpka Tea Party; Karen Kenney, founder of the San Fernando Valley Patriots; Sue Martinek, founder of the Coalition for Life of Iowa; Catherine Engelbrecht, president and founder of True the Vote and King Street Patriots; Amy Kremer, co-founder of the Tea Party Express; and Yvonne Donnelly, chair of The 9/12 Project.

Testifying before the House Ways and Means Committee about her intimidating experience with the IRS, Becky Gerritson broke down. "We don't understand why our government tried to stop us," Gerritson said. "I am not here today as a serf or a vassal. I am not begging my lords for mercy. I am a born-free, American woman— wife, mother and citizen—and I'm telling MY government that you have forgotten your place."

Gerritson added, "It is not your responsibility to look out for my well-being or monitor my speech. It is not your right to assert an agenda. The posts you occupy exist to preserve American liberty. You have sworn to perform that duty. And you have faltered."

Gerritson then explained the lengths the IRS went to in order to retrieve information. "I was asked to hand over my list of donors, including the amounts that they gave and the dates on which they gave them." The questions that were asked shocked her and were laced with intimidation, because "501c4 organizations do NOT have to disclose donor information."

Tea Party leaders were asked to identify volunteers, to provide content of speeches, educational forums, names of speeches, names of minors attending events, copies of written communications to legislators, and more. Eventually Tea Party attendants, including mothers, felt their safety and privacy was at risk. Some eventually gave up, fearing the consequences to their private lives. Julia Hodges, a Tea Party activist with the Mississippi Tea Party, withdrew the group's application for tax-exempt status after months of delays and intimidation.

Karen L. Kenney, a marriage and family therapist with a Ph.D., also gave up even trying to make the IRS do its job. "I stopped the costly and exhausting IRS process in July 2012. We survive on my credit card and donations in our cake tin," Kenney said. "To whisper the letters I-R-S strikes a shrill note on Main Street, U.S.A., but when this behemoth tramples upon America's grassroots, few hear the snapping sounds."

Catherine Engelbrecht, president of King Street Patriots and True the Vote, which advocates for voter ID laws, received unwanted attention not only from the IRS, but from a whole slew of federal agencies, including the FBI, ATF, and OSHA. In addition to being politically active, Engelbrecht owns a small business with her husband, and they hold a federal firearms license. In twenty years of business, she'd never seen any of those agencies until she applied for nonprofit C-3 status in early 2010 for True the Vote and King Street Patriots.

Authorities from each agency asked her hundreds and hundreds of strange, personal, and prying questions, which she was required to answer under the threat of perjury. There were seventeen rounds of questioning, with some stacks of "questionnaires" towering four inches in height. The IRS went so far as to ask for a record of everything she had ever put on Facebook or sent out on Twitter.[6] ATF showed up repeatedly to conduct audits of both her business and her family's personal safe for all the firearms.

Jenny Beth Martin is the founder of Tea Party Patriots, one of the largest national Tea Party organizations in the country. In 2010, *Time* magazine named her one of the one hundred most influential leaders in the world. Currently, Tea Party Patriots has eighteen hundred local chapters and more than 15 million members. She was also targeted by the IRS.

"We have on our staff, of the people who are active and who are not just employees but also activists, most of the people who are activists and on our staff are women and we have a lot of state coordinators who are women," Martin said in an interview.

The IRS asked Martin questions similar to the ones asked of Engelbrecht. The IRS wanted to know who in the media she was working with and sending press releases to, who was attending her events, and what was being posted on Facebook. In a similar case, the IRS demanded Marion Bower from American Patriots Against Government Excess provide a list of books read by the group, complete with a book report on each one.

"They have singled us out and discriminated and persecuted us. Government agents have used the IRS as a weapon to silence speech, harass innocent Americans and perhaps, sway elections," Martin said during a fiery speech in Washington during a protest of the IRS. "The damage the IRS has caused may be immeasurable."

"The women do run these groups," chairwoman of First State Tea Party in Delaware Cecile DiNozzi told me. "I think that it [IRS targeting] is an attack on women."

DiNozzi mentioned that her group's joint lawsuit against the IRS for targeting includes language from President Obama openly smearing Tea Party and patriot groups as people with "shadowy names" possibly "hiding behind foreign controlled entities."

"This is so wrong, we're everyday moms raising our families and the name calling and to insinuate I have something to do with a foreign entity is, I mean, that? My own government turning on me? It's unbelievable," DiNozzi said.

As the IRS continued their harassment of DiNozzi's groups and dragged their application for tax-exempt status out for as long as possible, donations and volunteers started to dry up, stunting their activity and impact in 2012.

"You do go through money and folks were generous the first year and the second year when we didn't hear from the IRS, they were getting a little nervous, 'What's going on?' And then those who had given us a little bit more than most, and one fellow purchased the computer that I used and that was a gift that he wrote off but if we didn't get that approval he would have had to re-file or do something with his tax return. So you know, people were talking and that's why I was even afraid to even move into the lawsuit against the IRS because how were people going to take it? Were they going to get more scared? Supportive? Things like that," she explained.

The good news is, everyone in DiNozzi's group applauded when she announced the lawsuit had been filed.

"Contrary to the blatant lies and smears propagated by left-wing politicians, activist groups, and their media allies, the Tea Party stands for liberty for all Americans. The proof of its inclusiveness can easily be found by looking at the leaders of both national and local organizations. Women played a central role in igniting this movement and they continue to provide leadership in its day-to-day operation," FreedomWorks Tea Party activist Deneen Borelli said to me. "As a black female conservative, my involvement in this grassroots movement dispels any myth surrounding the anti-women and anti-black claims by the left. Ironically, my national recognition as a conservative commentator was a result of having an opportunity to speak before a crowd of over eight hundred thousand at Freedom-Works' 2009 March on D.C."

Liberals always claim to want women to get involved in politics, but Obama's IRS had other plans for women who planned to oppose them on policy.

INDICTMENT 5: OBAMANOMICS

As former governor Mitt Romney told me in 2013, "The president's policies have made it harder for women to get good jobs, and the number-one issue we heard on the campaign trail from women of many different states was hoping they could find a good job, that their spouse might be able to do the same, and that their children could find good jobs when they come out of school. And this administration has been terribly disappointing in finding the kind of employment opportunities women were looking for."

Indeed, since the "greatest economic crisis since the Great Depression" in 2009, as Obama called it, the president has repeatedly used women to get Democrats and himself re-elected, but he hasn't done much to get women back to work. There are 780,000 fewer women in the workforce today than when President Obama took office in 2009. Joblessness for women under his watch has jumped 15.5 percent and over 92 percent of jobs lost have been lost by women, according the Bureau of Labor Statistics. It's been so bad for the female gender that the so-called recovery has been dubbed a "he-recovery" by economists and the National Women's Law Center, as jobs for men have come back at a faster pace than jobs for women (who voted Obama into office twice). From 2009 to 2011, women were the only group in America whose employment growth didn't keep up with population growth.[7]

But Obama's poor economic performance shouldn't be surprising, considering how he believes women should depend on government for nearly everything. Obama laid out his vision for government-dependent women during his 2012 campaign in a slideshow called "The Life of Julia" (previously mentioned in Chapter 2). The gist of the "Julia" campaign was a propaganda push to show female voters how Obama's policies would "help" them through life, starting at the cradle and ending at the grave.

"The Life of Julia" started out in the public education system. "Under President Obama: Julia is enrolled in a Head Start program to help her get ready for school. Because of steps President Obama has taken to improve programs like this one, Julia joins thousands of students across the country who will start kindergarten ready to learn and succeed."

Got that? Without Obama dumping millions into the education system, Julia would be a complete failure.

Fast-forward to high school, and Julia is seventeen and ready for college thanks to Race to the Top, a program implemented by President Obama. "Under President Obama: Julia takes the SAT and is on track to start her college applications. Her high school is part of the Race to the Top program, implemented by President Obama. Their new college—and—career-ready standards mean Julia can take the classes she needs to do well." Again, without Barack Obama's big government, Julia would be a failure.

When she becomes a legal adult on her way to college, Julia is able to take advantage of a tax credit. Thanks to Barack Obama. "Under President Obama: As she prepares for her first semester of college, Julia and her family qualify for President Obama's American

Opportunity Tax Credit—worth up to $10,000 over four years. Julia is also one of millions of students who receive a Pell Grant to help put a college education within reach."

Then, after she graduates, "Julia's federal student loans are more manageable since President Obama capped income-based federal student loan payments and kept interest rates low. She makes her payments on time every month, keeping her on track to repay her student loans."

The problem with this scenario is that youth unemployment under Barack Obama has consistently hovered around 16 percent, and that only includes young people who haven't given up looking for a job to start their career. Without a job, student loans are impossible to pay back, which is why America is facing a $1 trillion student loan crisis.

Next, Julia is old enough to take advantage of Barack Obama's signature failure—Obamacare. She's also able to become an adult-child by staying on her parents' health insurance until she's twenty-six. "Under President Obama: During college Julia undergoes surgery and is thankfully covered by her insurance due to a provision in health-care reform that allows her to stay on her parents' insurance until she turns twenty-six years-old."

When she goes to work after college (unlike the 16 percent of young Americans who can't find a job in Obama's economy), she's protected by the Lilly Ledbetter Fair Pay Act, making her "one of millions of women across the country who knows she'll always be able to stand up for her equal right of equal pay." And "thanks to Obamacare, her health insurance is required to cover birth control and preventive care, letting Julia focus on her work rather than worry about her health."

What in the world would Julia do if she had to "worry" about things like birth control? After all, Obamacare makes it "free." I'm just not sure how American women went about preventing pregnancy and staying healthy in the decades before Obamacare. How did women move forward? How did the human race move forward? That nine dollars per month for pills was *really* a threat to the survival of women everywhere!

Julia is now in her thirties, and it looks as if she's stopped taking her free birth control. "Under President Obama: Julia's son Zachary starts kindergarten. The public schools in their neighborhood have better facilities and great teachers because of President Obama's investments in education and programs like Race to the Top."

In case you were wondering, Zachary doesn't have a father in "The Life of Julia." The campaign pushed single parenthood, which in turn pushes women further into poverty. According to the Heritage Foundation, 71 percent of poor parents with one or more children are not married. "According to the U.S. Census, the poverty rate for single parents with children in the United States in 2009 was 37.1 percent. The rate for married couples with children was 6.8 percent. Being raised in a married family reduced a child's probability of living in poverty by about 82 percent."[8]

In addition, children without fathers, like Zachary, are more likely to end up in prison or drop out of school, as well as being more prone to drug abuse and suicide. The vast majority of teenagers locked up in juvenile detention centers were raised only by their mothers. In his slide show, Obama also failed to mention the cost of single mothers like Julia to the taxpayer: more than $110 billion per year.

Moving on, after working as a web designer as an employee for years, Julia is now starting her own business. "Under President Obama: Julia starts her own Web business. She qualifies for a Small Business Administration loan, giving her the money she needs to invest in her business. President Obama's tax cuts for small businesses like Julia's help her to get started. She's able to hire employees, creating new jobs in her town and helping to grow the local economy."

Oops! Obama didn't tell Julia that her taxes would be going up as a small business owner if she makes more than $250,000 per year, which means less money in her pocket, less money to hire employees, less money to create jobs, and less growth in the economy.

Finally, after a long life of hand-holding from the government, Julia is ready to retire. Throughout "The Life of Julia," savings and a 401(k) plan are never mentioned, but don't worry, Medicare and Social Security are there to save the day! "Under President Obama: Julia enrolls in Medicare, helping her to afford preventive care and the prescription drugs she needs.... After years of contributing to Social Security, she receives monthly benefits that help her retire comfortably, without worrying that she'll run out of savings. This allows her to volunteer at a community garden."

Julia wasn't told that she'll also need to grow her *own* food at the community garden, too, because there won't be enough money through Social Security to pay for rising food costs. Barack Obama's telling women like "Julia" they can live "comfortably" in retirement on Social Security and Medicare is a big lie and complete distortion of reality. If Julia was three when Barack Obama first took office and Julia retires at sixty-seven, Medicare and Social Security will have gone broke a very long time ago. In the year 2013, both programs faced $63 trillion in long-term deficits. Half of that amount is up for payment during Julia's life and before her retirement. Moreover, it's the progressive "Julia" policies Obama sells to women that are the reason Social Security and Medicare will no longer be available unless they are reformed, something the president isn't willing to do.

"The Life of Julia" is not one of big government bliss or "pro-women policies." Instead, it's one of disappointment, hopeless dependency, and broken promises. Obama's deliberate posturing to young women through the use of "Julia" should be noted. Why didn't we ever see "The Life of John"? It's apparent Team Obama sees only women, not men, as helpless victims of their gender needy of government assistance to survive every stage of life.

INDICTMENT 6: OBAMACARE

When President Obama was running for re-election in 2012, women voters in swing states said their number-one concern was health care, according to Gallup polling. For years, Barack Obama had been out on the campaign trail promising his signature piece of legislation would be good for women, would provide better health care for women, and would lower costs by making "being a woman no longer a pre-existing condition." Obama was able to influence younger women voters by claiming birth control would be free. But sadly, Barack Obama ended up like so many other guys: full of broken promises and heartache.

As Obamacare began its train wreck of a rollout on October 1, 2013, women began to see they had been lied to. The cost of health insurance for many women skyrocketed, making those nine-dollar birth control pills before Obamacare look pretty cheap. According to the Manhattan Institute, Obamacare is increasing women's rates by 62 percent nationally, and depending on the state, some women could see their premiums triple.[9] In addition, millions of women have received letters stating their insurance plans are being canceled because they do not comply with the Affordable Care Act.

Obama promised women otherwise. "If you like your doctor," he said, "you will be able to keep your doctor. Period. If you like your health-care plan, you will be able to keep your health-care plan. Period. No one will take it away. No matter what."

Shortly after the disastrous Obamacare exchanges launched on October 1, 2013, a woman named Edie Littlefield Sundby from California lost her doctor and her health insurance as a result of the new health-care overhaul. Sundby is living with stage-4 gallbladder cancer. She had great doctors and great coverage. Now, she doesn't.

"Everyone now is clamoring about Affordable Care Act winners and losers. I am one of the losers. My grievance is not political; all my energies are directed to enjoying life and staying alive, and I have no time for politics. For almost seven years I have fought and survived stage-4 gallbladder cancer, with a five-year survival rate of less than 2% after diagnosis. I am a determined fighter and extremely lucky. But this luck may have just run out: My affordable, lifesaving medical insurance policy has been canceled effective Dec. 31. My choice is to get coverage through the government health exchange and lose access to my cancer doctors, or pay much more for insurance outside the exchange (the quotes average 40% to 50% more) for the privilege of starting over with an unfamiliar insurance company and impaired benefits," Sundby wrote in the *Wall Street Journal*.[10] "After four weeks of researching plans on the website, talking directly to government exchange counselors, insurance companies and medical providers, my insurance broker and I are as confused as ever. Time is running out and we still don't have a clue how to best proceed."

When the White House got wind of Sundby's situation and when the press started asking questions about Obamacare's forcing the cancellation of her coverage, *Think Progress*, headed by former Clinton advisor and current Obama advisor John Podesta, mocked her and justified the cancellation of her plan.

"Sundby shouldn't blame reform," the article stated. "Sundby is losing her coverage and her doctors because of a business decision her insurer made within the competitive dynamics of California's health care market. She'll now have to enroll in a new plan that offers tighter networks of providers as a way to control health care costs and offer lower premiums."

Further, White House communications director Dan Pfeiffer flippantly tweeted the *Think Progress* hit piece. Obama's minions promised Sundby would get better, more affordable coverage. She hasn't and she won't. Another woman, Debra Fishericks of Virginia, lost her health insurance thanks to Obamacare. Fishericks is fighting kidney cancer and can't afford any of the health-care plans available in the government exchanges.

More generally speaking, for women, health care can be more intimate than the health care of a man. It isn't easy for women to find a gynecologist they are comfortable with, and it's not exactly something you want to go "shopping for." Regardless, millions of women don't have a choice now. Obamacare specifically tells women which doctors they can go to and where. If their previous doctor—the one they were told they could keep—doesn't fit into Obamacare's criteria, well, that's just too bad.

Obamacare is especially bad for married women who relied on their husbands' health insurance plans. Thanks to Obamacare's costs, many companies have been forced to cut spousal health insurance, meaning that male employees' wives have only the option of high-priced Obamacare exchanges. In addition, dependent coverage for children is also being dropped due to soaring costs to companies. According to the Kaiser Family Foundation, health-care premiums for families have gone up by at least three thousand dollars per year, not down by twenty-five hundred dollars as President Obama promised.

Women working good part-time jobs with health-care benefits

are also suffering under Obamacare. They've found those benefits, and their hours, stripped away by new regulations.

Even Patti Davis, President Ronald Reagan's liberal activist daughter, was surprised when she was told she would be losing her health plan. "Could the president please explain why I and others are losing our health ins. plans? Wasn't supposed to happen!" Davis tweeted three weeks after the Obamacare rollout.

The evidence against Obamacare is not just anecdotal. Study after study has shown its disastrous effect. For example, according to a study[11] by the American Action Forum, "There were no decreases in 2014 premium rates for healthy, 30 year old women under the exchange system as compared to the individual market in 2013." Instead, every state in the union "saw insurance rate increases, with 42 of those states experiencing triple digit percentage increases in premiums for the lowest-priced coverage."

It's a good thing "Julia" was born during Obama's administration, and not thirty years before it. The American Action Forum's study says, "Pre-ACA premiums for a 30 year old nonsmoking woman average $74.49 monthly, while post-ACA premiums average $188.72 per month, a $114.23, or 153 percent, increase. The average percent change between 2013 and 2014 minimum level plan monthly premiums is 193 percent, reflecting a nearly 2 to 1 ratio between the two sets of premiums."

These numbers add up to anything but "free," "high-quality" and "less expensive" coverage when it comes to women's health-care plans.

INDICTMENT 7: NEGOTIATING WITH IRAN

As a presidential candidate, Barack Obama didn't know much about foreign policy. He'd barely been a senator for five minutes, and he didn't get a lot of international-relations experience as a community organizer. But there was one big, bold diplomatic initiative that made Obama stand out: He wanted to negotiate with Iran.

Iran, of course, is among the most anti-women regimes in the world. According to an ex-CIA spy who lived a double life in Iran, the Iranian regime has subjected women to "the cruelest of punishments" ever since the 1979 Islamic Revolution. One of the regime's first orders "was to force all women to wear the Islamic hijab, covering their hair and their body." Disobedience to the law is punished severely, and "thousands of innocent young girls have been brought to prison for the most specious of reasons," such as dressing immodestly or flirting before marriage.

The ex-spy reports, "Every few days, guards call out names over a loudspeaker. These women know what it means to have their names called, and they hold hands, praying that this will not be the day they are dragged out of their cell and executed. Those whose names are not called for execution are lined up and lashed. Many of them faint from the lashing, never knowing what the guards do with their unconscious bodies. If they are called, they are raped before execution so they are no longer virgins and therefore, according to hard-line Islamic beliefs, can no longer go to heaven."

The girls who are raped and executed were denied the opportunity to "ever know the joys of romantic love. None of them would ever hold her own baby in her arms. Their final days have been filled with a level of abuse few can imagine." And even those who follow Iran's medieval laws are subject to the regime's barbaric cruelty. "Many women—sometimes as young as fifteen—have been stoned to death on bogus charges of adultery."

What is Barack Obama's response to this regime? He gave little to no support to Iranian protesters who risked their lives—and sometimes lost their lives—opposing the corrupt presidency of Mahmoud Ahmadinejad in the Green Movement of 2009. Instead, he has extended olive branches to Iranian leaders and insisted on negotiating with the leaders of one of the world's most heinous— and most anti-women—regimes. Fast-forward to 2011 and 2012 when we saw President Obama openly support the Arab Spring and Mohammed Morsi of the Muslim Brotherhood to head Egypt as president. Morsi, who has since been taken out of office, is part of the same Muslim Brotherhood responsible for the rape, disrespect, and genital mutilation of women across the globe. Rape under Morsi, and during the Arab Spring overall, was described as an epidemic.[12]

When you have candidates like John F. Kennedy and Woodrow Wilson, a title like "the Most Anti-Woman President in American History" can't be bestowed lightly. The competition is stiff. But the facts are what they are. When it comes to Barack Obama, it isn't what he does to a few women, it's what he does to *all* women. It's about how he objectifies them as pawns of government, as second-class citizens whose husbands and boyfriends have been replaced by Washington, D.C. The patronizing and condescending tone of Obama's "Life of Julia" campaign said it all. We are nothing without big government. We are nothing without him.

Obama's rhetoric as a self-appointed champion for women everywhere is belied by a record that is hostile to all self-respecting females who pride themselves on independence. After all, isn't that supposedly what feminism is all about?

Somewhere modern liberalism betrayed the original values of feminism about empowerment and choice.

Part III

THE WOMEN THEY DON'T WANT YOU TO KNOW

CHAPTER 9

THE ABORTION LIE

Many women will tell you that abortion is the main reason they vote for Democrats. They'll say that the Democratic Party's "pro-choice" platform is the best thing about the party of Jackson and Franklin Roosevelt. They'll excuse every Democratic politician's scandals, lies, and abuse of women in their personal lives just because that politician vows to protect the right to an abortion any time, any place, for any reason.

Mitt Romney learned this lesson firsthand. When I interviewed him for this book, he said, "As long as the candidate of our party is going to be a right-to-life candidate, then Democrats will seek to say that that is an anti-women, anti-woman position."

As a husband, he had been instrumental in supporting his wife, Ann, through multiple sclerosis, but because he didn't support abortion, he was routinely slandered as waging a war on women's health. He told me that "women are often in disagreement" about abortion rights "and many of the leading right to life advocates in America are in fact women." Nevertheless, "The Democrats have tried to use that as a wedge and will probably continue to do so."

The irony is that the Democratic Party's embrace of abortion is one of the biggest reasons why the party is awful for women. (It's also pretty bad for the estimated 650,000 unborn girls who are aborted every year, but that's not the topic of this chapter.) Back in the day, feminists were against abortion because they felt that it gave men an opportunity to exploit women as objects simply for sexual pleasure without having to deal with the responsibility of sex. Today, feminists are pro-abortion in the name of women's choice, while keeping the truth about abortion from women, putting them at risk for a life of regret and depression.

Whether you're pro-abortion or anti-abortion, it's important that we have an honest conversation about what abortion really is. Pregnancy is not a disease, and according to scientific standards, abortion ends life and has a damaging long-term effect on women. It isn't harmless, as women's rights groups would have many women, mostly young, believe.

In June 2013, the year of *Roe v. Wade*'s fortieth anniversary, CNN asked online readers two questions: Have you had an abortion? If so, how do you feel about it now? The responses to those questions were telling. Hundreds of women, 539 of them,[1] sent in responses, and the overwhelming majority of them detailed the grief and regret they feel about their abortions. Titles for submissions included "Until we meet again," "soul deep ache," and "I never got over it."

One woman, named Tricia Helfin, wrote:[2]

Abortion is sold as a woman's right. A solution to unwanted pregnancy. A quick procedure that once over, never has to be thought about again. I chose abortion at 18 years old. Now, 37 years later, I certainly have not forgotten. We are told that a woman has the right to control her own body as if abortion is a means of control. Once chosen, abortion creates its own effects. The physical, emotional, and psychological effects are beyond our control. Abortion does what it is designed to do. . . . Kill and destroy; abruptly halt an ongoing process . . . the process of LIFE. No woman is ever freed by abortion. The only partner in the conception who can "walk" is the man. There is no glory in this choice. Abortion is NOT for women it is AGAINST us.

President of Abortion Recovery InterNational Stacy Massey submitted a response[3] about her experience with people who have been associated with abortion:

Abortion Affects Everything. It impacts our marriages and our most intimate bonds with each other.

But it goes deeper than that. We as a society, don't know how to respond. Families are not talking about the subject matter. Not because they don't want to, but because they don't know what to say or how to say it. Many times, parents themselves may be hurting from their own abortion experience. And so the cycle of silent pain continues . . . their children have abortions and so on, and so on. Friends drive each other to the clinic and then never speak about it again. This "surgery" literally changes a person's life forever . . . and we are suddenly mute. We receive over 100 requests PER DAY from individuals and families looking for after abortion help. Over 250,000 hurting people have contacted us just in the last 5 years.

Natja Osborn and Teresa Small also have a story. They're both a product of the abortion giant's lies, and after two decades of living with the painful feelings of guilt that follow an abortion, both are pro-life activists determined to provide women with the information about abortion that abortion doctors and clinics won't give them.

They are the kind of women Planned Parenthood doesn't want you to know about.

NATJA'S STORY

It was July 21, 1992, when Natja Osborn, who is from Germany, stepped into an abortion clinic in Holland at the age of twenty-one. She was in an abusive marriage at the time. She was cheated on, verbally and physically abused, and her husband told her that if she ever left him, she would never see her child. She felt as if her only way out was through abortion.

"I was thirteen weeks, but even at thirteen weeks I was told that it's not life yet. I remember that: 'It's not life yet,'" Natja told me. "After seeing my doctor he told me that Germany had a nine-week cut-off period; however, Holland is without limitations. I was never advised to seek any other help (abuse help center, psychologist, etc.). I went to Holland with my brother. The trip there was full of emotions; however, I felt more anger than anything else. Anger because I thought that was the only way," she told me, with anger still in her voice.

"We entered the room, and the doctor didn't ask me why I was doing it," Osborn says. "He only asked me if I wanted the procedure with full anesthesia or partial, noting it would cost extra. I was asked to see the baby [asked to view an ultrasound of the baby in the womb]. I took a very quick peek and saw a full-size baby. I felt it move. After I looked away they put me under."

Not once did a doctor talk to Natja about the emotional costs of the abortion. Instead, "They were laughing with each other as if it was no big deal. After I woke up, nobody came to see me. My brother was with me. I was in the room with other women, and we all cried."

When Natja left the clinic, she felt as though the procedure hadn't happened. She felt fine physically and didn't have any side effects until a week later, when she experienced extreme pain and blood clots. Those side effects were nothing, however, compared to the emotional devastation she felt in the years that followed.

Today, Natja can think of many questions she wished she had been encouraged to ask herself before aborting the child inside her: "Am I doing the right thing? Is there any other way?" She wishes she had been told how the procedure would be done, how her body would change afterward, and how difficult it would subsequently be to carry another child. Natja eventually married again and suffered three miscarriages as a result of her abortion, another damaging and depressing experience. She says her regret "will never go away."

Natja also says that abortion is "all about money and making money," and as a school health aide in a middle school, Natja saw how groups like Planned Parenthood filled their pockets by preying on young girls in the public school system. "In my health office there were flyers in the middle school about Planned Parenthood," she says. "I looked at my principal and I said, 'What is this? We're at a middle school, we're talking about sixth-, seventh-, and eighth-graders.' And she said, 'Well in case somebody came in here pregnant.' They wanted me to send children to Planned Parenthood. I said I wasn't going to promote it and that it wasn't going to happen."

TERESA'S STORY

"I'll try to do it without crying," Teresa told me when I asked her to tell me about her abortion twenty years ago.

When Teresa became pregnant, she was unmarried and was told by her boyfriend that she needed an abortion. She was twelve weeks pregnant, which means her child had a heart, stomach, kidneys, fingers, fingerprints, a mouth it could open and a face that looked like a baby's.[4]

"What I can remember is I approached Planned Parenthood in my town and they really didn't give me much information other than they set me up for an appointment and said I was going to need to go to San Diego," she recalls. "I was so confused in my state I really didn't realize until many years after, what I did."

Teresa feels "lied to" by people who were determined to prevent her from changing her mind. "It was almost as if it was intentionally done." She says no one at Planned Parenthood said, "Maybe you want to think about this a little bit more and here are some other things you might want to consider. . . . When someone becomes pregnant they need to know their only option isn't to abort. That the option is, which is a better choice, is putting the child up for adoption. If I could do things all over again I would have had my child. I would not have had an abortion."

Two decades after the procedure, Teresa is still dealing with postpartum depression, and it wasn't until just two years ago that she was able to forgive herself. Only after a retreat with a support group for women who've had abortions, called Rachel's Vineyard, was Teresa finally able to let go and move forward.

Rachel's Vineyard was started in 1994 by Dr. Teresa Karminski Burke to help women heal from the pain and long-term emotional, psychological, and physical complications that come from an abortion.

The Rachel's Vineyard retreat helped Teresa understand that "God is an awesome and forgiving God and that I could still receive forgiveness from him." She says, "The other step is also forgiving oneself."

Often, women who have abortions go through the entire process alone, but according to Teresa, "In order to truly heal, you do need to share, because by witnessing you're able to let others see that they might be going through that same thing, or affected in that same way."

Unfortunately, most women who are considering an abortion have no idea about the anguish that Teresa has had to live with and overcome. Instead, as Teresa puts it, "Society as a whole has been brainwashed." Women don't understand, until it's too late, "that it's not just a blob of tissue, it's your child."

A LACK OF INFORMATION

Women's rights groups often portray abortion as empowering for the female gender. But as Dorinda Bordlee, vice president of the Bio-Ethics Defense Fund, told the 2013 National Review Institute Summit, the opposite is true:

> Women find themselves in abortion clinics because they are either abandoned by the men who should be loving them instead of using them, or they are coerced either physically or otherwise by either the men in their lives or often sadly their parents. Abortion is a place of hopelessness....
>
> The reason why we have so much success in the states as far as regulating abortion is the voices of very courageous post-abortive women who can speak to this and speak to the lie of what abortion has done to destroy their psychological lives, their relationships, that horrible medical impact which I could give you a mountain of data....
>
> I'm blessed with four children. Three of them are teenagers and young adults, and as they look at what's going on, they're

saying, "You know, they keep shoving these contraceptives, abor-
tifacient drugs, abortion, do they think we're prostitutes? Are
we here just to be used? As somebody's great date?" There's no
respect, there is no respect that young women are looking for.
We are made to love and be loved not to use and be used. This
administration wants us to think we are here to be used and we
are not.

If Democratic politicians truly cared about women, they would tell
Planned Parenthood and other pro-abortion lobbyists there's nothing "pro-choice" about their opposition to informed consent. Those
groups consistently fight against informed consent before abortion,
because when women realize what they're about to do, they often
change their minds and carry their child to term, which means the
abortion clinic, and the industry as a whole, loses money.

Consider, for example, the sign Louisiana now requires abortion
clinics to post in waiting and operating rooms:

Women: Know Your Rights www.pregnancyinfo.LA.gov.
You can't be forced: It is unlawful for anyone to make you have an
abortion against your will, even if you are a minor.

You are not alone: Many public and private agencies are willing to help
you carry your child to term and to assist after your child's birth.

You and the father: The father of your child is liable to assist in the
support of your child even if he has offered to pay for the abortion.

You and adoption: The law allows adoptive parents to pay costs of
prenatal care, childbirth and newborn care.

During a meeting of the committee considering the legislation requiring the "Know Your Rights" sign, a Planned Parenthood lobbyist objected to the signs, saying they were "offensive to women." When the lobbyist was asked to point out specifically what part of the sign was offensive, she didn't give a direct answer and eventually said the sign was offensive because "most women already know these things."

No, they don't. Every other medical procedure, whether it's getting your teeth cleaned, a physical exam, vaccinations, major surgery, or even picking up a prescription at the pharmacy, requires informed consent of patients. You can't watch an advertisement for medicine without hearing a litany of possible side effects. But when it comes to the emotional and physical side effects of an abortion, Planned Parenthood doesn't want you to hear about them.

THE HOOK-UP CULTURE

In order to properly address the long-term damaging effects of abortion on women, it's impossible not to address the hook-up culture that leads to an abortion culture. Depression doesn't start in the abortion clinic; it starts in the bedroom after casual sex, which has been openly promoted by women's rights groups since the 1960s.

A 2013 joint study from the University of California–Los Angeles and the University of Texas shows that women normally regret sleeping with men who aren't monogamous or caring partners. The study also showed women regret moving too quickly in a sexual manner with a new partner and losing virginity to the wrong partner. "The consequences of casual sex were so much higher for women than for men, and this is likely to have shaped emotional reactions to sexual liaisons," UCLA psychology professor Martie Haselton said in an interview with Reuters about the study.

Another study from Ohio State University[5] found casual sex, defined by the absence of a relationship and just the act of sex, can lead to depression and even thoughts of suicide. "Several studies have found a link between poor mental health and casual sex, but the nature of that association has been unclear," lead author of the study Dr. Sara Sandberg-Thoma told the *Daily Mail*.[6] "This study provides evidence that poor mental health can lead to casual sex, but also that casual sex leads to additional declines in mental health." The study also showed casual sex leads to depression in men, too, which undermines the feminist argument that women should have detached, impersonal "sex like men."

Despite casual sex being promoted by women's rights groups and Hollywood as adventurous and fulfilling, it isn't. So what is? Married sex. *Gasp*. A 2010 study from the Center for Sexual Health Promotion at Indiana University showed married couples have more sex than single people, more adventurous sex, and more fulfilling sex. Another 2006 global study[7] from the *British Medical Journal* showed the same. It's amazing what can happen when someone actually cares about you as a person, not as a casual sex object.

When Princeton University alum Susan Patton wrote an op-ed in the *Daily Princetonian* suggesting young women find a good, respectful man while they're in college, the women's lobby was up in arms. Their outrage was surprising to me, considering loving partners are scientifically proven to be better for women's health and better for satisfactory sex (and more of it, too).

It would seem Patton's haters, promoting the opposite of monogamy and a solid lifelong relationship, think women should emulate the hook-up-loving characters of HBO's *Girls* while they're young instead of thinking about a possible married future, and Democratic leaders are only too happy to cheer them on. Even President Obama has gotten in on the act. On October 25, 2012, just days before the presidential election, *Girls'* Lena Dunham appeared in a promotional video for Obama for America. The subject matter? Your first time.

Dunham, dressed in a white T-shirt and wearing a statement necklace, gave direct advice to girls all over America:

> Your first time shouldn't be with just anybody. You want to do it with a great guy. It should be with a guy with beautiful . . . someone who really cares about and understands women. A guy who cares when you get health insurance and specifically whether you get birth control. The consequences are huge. You wanna do it with a guy who brought the troops out of Iraq. You don't want a guy who says, "Oh, hey I'm at the library studying," when really he's not out signing the Lilly Ledbetter Act. Or who thinks that gay people should never have beautiful complicated weddings like the kind we see on Bravo or TLC all the time. It's a fun game to say, "Who are you voting for?" and they say, "I don't want to tell you." And you say, "No who are you voting for?" and they go, "Guess." Think about how you want to spend those four years. In college age time, that's 150 years. It's also super uncool to be out and about when someone says, "Did you vote?" "Nah, I wasn't ready." My first time voting was . . . amazing. It was this line in the sand. Before I was a girl, now I was a woman. I went to the polling station, I pulled back the curtain, I voted for Barack Obama.

If you thought Dunham was referring to a young girl losing her virginity, don't worry, that was the point. In Dunham's world, it doesn't matter if your "first time" is with someone who deeply respects you as a person. It's just important for him to be a "beautiful" guy who "understands women" and cares "whether you get birth control." (According to New York City voter files, Dunham didn't even actually vote on Election Day, when she was in India. According to Dunham, she voted by affidavit through her father.)

As Dunham's video shows, the culture of casual free "love" that was spawned out of the 1960s is alive and well today with a dash of modern snark to water down the meaning of sex and loss of virginity. But for women especially, that "love" isn't free and the snark isn't actually watering down anything. Scientific studies prove it. The hook-up and abortion culture leads to depression, embraces a patriarchy feminists claim to be fighting against, and puts men in positions of power over women.

PLANNED PARENTHOOD'S WAR ON WOMEN'S HEALTH

Abortion advocates often claim they believe in safe health environments for women. Bill Clinton once said abortion should be "safe, legal, and rare." But these days, the abortion lobby has given up any pretense of wanting abortion to be "rare," and by opposing safety regulations for abortion clinics, they've sacrificed any interest in "safe" abortions.

One needs to look no further than horrific conditions of clinics run by abortion practitioners like Kermit Gosnell, as briefly discussed earlier.

A specialist in late-term abortions, Gosnell operated a clinic in Philadelphia, inaptly named the Women's Medical Society. It went uninspected for nearly two decades thanks to pro-abortion advocates repeatedly blocking legislation that would regulate abortion clinics. As a result, Gosnell killed countless full-term babies and immigrant

Karnamaya Mongar. Over a thirty-year period, Gosnell performed thousands of abortions, charging women hundreds, even thousands of dollars, making him rich. The man is America's worst serial killer.

After a lengthy trial in 2013, in which witnesses and clinic workers described Gosnell snipping the backs of babies that he said could "walk me to the bus stop," Gosnell was convicted of killing three full-term babies and causing the death of a patient. Ironically although Gosnell was African-American, he had two separate rooms for abortion, one for minorities and one for white women (the cleaner one), because he thought minorities would be less likely to complain.

Gosnell's clinic was described as a "house of horrors," with blood on the walls, tools, and floor. He kept jars and cabinets of baby feet in his office, stuffed babies in the freezer, and allowed cats to urinate all over the place. A stench of urine filled the air. Abortions were performed by clinic workers who had little to no medical training, and baby parts were put down the garbage disposal in the clinic sink. "The smells were just unbearable," one investigator said. "You could tell there was death somewhere. Opening up the cabinet and seeing all the feet. I'll remember that for a long time."[8]

When the horrific details became public, the Democratic Party and the mainstream media did their best to ignore the story, sanitize it, or in some instances, cover up their possible complicity in it. The three major television networks chose to ignore the story, and when the *New York Times* finally decided to cover the story, the paper referred to full-term healthy babies killed outside the womb as "fetuses removed from their mothers."

On the day of Gosnell's conviction, the National Abortion Rights Action League blamed Gosnell's horrors on legislation requiring clinic inspections. "The numbers don't lie—restricting abortion access puts women in danger," said NARAL. "The guilty verdict in the trial of Kermit Gosnell shows why we must continue to protect and expand access to safe, legal abortion care."

Like NARAL, Planned Parenthood advocated for more abortion. The organization's vice president for communications, Eric Ferrero, said, "This case has made clear that we must have and enforce laws that protect access to safe and legal abortion, and we must reject misguided laws that would limit women's options and force them to seek treatment from criminals like Kermit Gosnell."

Planned Parenthood's attempt at outrage was anything but sincere. Gosnell isn't alone in running unsafe abortion clinics, and Planned Parenthood is guilty of protecting them.

Early in 2013, two former nurses at a Planned Parenthood clinic in Delaware quit. They told a local news outlet[9] that conditions in the clinic were unsafe and unsanitary, and that the clinic did not undergo regular inspections. "It was just unsafe," one nurse told WPVI reporter Wendy Saltzman. "I couldn't tell you how ridiculously unsafe it was." Another nurse added, "They were using instruments on patients that were not sterile." Women were required to lie on soiled tables, potentially exposing them to lifelong diseases like AIDS and hepatitis.

"Planned Parenthood cannot claim to be truly concerned for women's health while at the same time opposing laws aimed at securing women's safety inside abortion clinics," pro-life Susan B. Anthony List president Marjorie Dannenfelser said in a statement at the time about the Delaware clinic. "America's number one abortion business cannot claim that the Kermit Gosnell 'house of horrors' is an isolated incident while their own employees expose them for conditions they call 'ridiculously unsafe.' The abortion industry cannot be relied upon to police themselves and repeatedly opposing efforts to strengthen health and safety standards in abortion clinics does not reflect true concern for women and girls."

Ellen Barosse, founder of the Delaware pro-life group A Rose and a Prayer added, "Delaware has a grisly history on abortion. Kermit Gosnell, now on trial in Philadelphia for the murder of infants born alive, practiced in Wilmington at the Atlantic Women's Medical Center for years, as did two of those testifying against him. It is a tragedy that in the state where we have the highest abortion rate in the country, these abortion clinics are not even subject to routine inspection. 'Safe, legal, and rare' has long been the mantra of the abortion industry and its supporters. It's clear that in Delaware only legal matters—patient safety is not a concern."

In the wake of the Gosnell scandal, the Texas legislature took up legislation with new clinic requirements: Clinics must meet higher health standards, doctors providing abortions must have admitting privileges to a nearby hospital in the case of an emergency, clinics must meet safety regulations of a surgical center, and doctors, not nurses, must administer abortion-inducing drugs. In response, the pro-abortion crowd cried—pardon the expression—bloody murder. Pro-abortion darling Wendy Davis became a national sensation overnight after a twelve-hour filibuster opposing the bill and a twenty-week late-term abortion ban. When Davis was later asked about her opinion on the Gosnell case, which sparked the Texas legislation, Davis pleaded ignorance and said she didn't know who he was.

THE WAR ON GIRLS

In China, abortion is used to weed out girls from the population. More female babies are aborted each year in China than are born in the United States. It is estimated there are more than 163 million "missing women" from Asia as a result of sex-selective abortion. "We are listening to people championing feminism?" asked Chuck Donovan of the Charlotte Lozier Institute during a panel discussion at the 2013 National Review Institute Summit. "While they're wiping out as many girls per year in the People's Republic of China as are born in the United States every year?"

Sadly, gendercide isn't an issue that is simply isolated in communist China. It's happening here in the United States.

In May 2012, the investigative group Live Action released a video showing a Planned Parenthood worker in an Austin, Texas, clinic helping a potential patient who wanted to abort if her child was a girl. In response to the investigation, Planned Parenthood called the incident "isolated." The same scenario played out in abortion clinics in Hawaii, New York, Arizona, and North Carolina.

A study[10] produced by Professor Jason Abrevaya at the University of Texas shows thousands of girls are missing in the United States thanks to sex-selective abortion and traditions of favoring boys being carried into the United States by Asian immigrants:

> We offer evidence of gender selection within the United States. Analysis of comprehensive birth data shows unusually high boy-birth percentages after 1980 among later children (most notably third and fourth children) born to Chinese and Asian Indian mothers. Based upon linked data from California, Asian Indian mothers are found to be significantly more likely to have a terminated pregnancy and to give birth to a boy when they have previously only given birth to girls. The observed boy-birth percentages are consistent with over 2,000 "missing" Chinese and Indian girls in the United States between 1991 and 2004.

When abortion clinics aren't busy promoting gendercide, they're busy covering up statutory rape of young girls. A 2009 investigation by the pro-life group Live Action showed eight clinics in five different states willing to cover up the sexual abuse and statutory rape of girls under the age of eighteen. Workers in Indiana, Arizona, Alabama, Tennessee, Wisconsin, and Kentucky are shown in a series of videos providing instructions to adult sexual predators about how to avoid parental consent laws.

Take, for example, a video of Lila Rose, president of Live Action, at an Indiana Planned Parenthood clinic. Rose pretended to be a minor and told a clinic worker that the man who got her pregnant "might be a lot older but he doesn't act a lot older, ya know?" Rose added, "He might be thirty-one."

The Planned Parenthood worker was determined to help Rose get an abortion, even if it meant covering up statutory rape. "It doesn't matter," said the worker. "I didn't hear the age ... I don't want to know the age." The worker then proceeded to help Rose lie about her boyfriend's age on her forms and evade parental consent laws.

Similarly, at a Planned Parenthood clinic in Tucson, a fifteen-year-old investigator told the clinic worker her boyfriend was not a minor and that he was twenty-seven. The worker said, "Don't tell me."

It is illegal to cover up statutory rape in fifty states, and clinic workers are required by law to report sexual abuse. But Planned Parenthood has repeatedly failed to report it. Instead, they habitually and unapologetically break the law.

Based on Planned Parenthood workers' support for sex-selective abortions and refusal to comply with parental consent and child-protection laws, it's no surprise the group has opposed laws against gender-selective abortion and requiring parental consent for abortions on children under eighteen.

The Democrats are right that there is a war on women's health. They're just wrong about who's waging the war. It is Planned Parenthood that has time and again fought against protections of women, especially young women. And it is the Democratic Party that has insisted on funding Planned Parenthood with federal tax dollars and that has defended Planned Parenthood's anti-woman agenda over and over again.

CHAPTER 10

HOLLYWOOD HATES WOMEN

In Hollywood a girl's virtue is much less important than her hairdo. You're judged by how you look, not by what you are. Hollywood's a place where they'll pay you a thousand dollars for a kiss, and fifty cents for your soul. I know, because I turned down the first offer enough and held out for the fifty cents.

—*Marilyn Monroe*

Do you know Samantha Geimer? You should, despite the powers-that-be in the $30-billion-a-year film industry not wanting you to. On March 10, 1977, at Jack Nicholson's house on the tony Mulholland Drive, she became one of liberal Hollywood's many victims in its war on women.

The encounter that afternoon with renowned film director Roman Polanski would forever change the thirteen-year-old Geimer's life. "We did photos with me drinking champagne," she said. According to court records, Geimer was also given a Quaalude.

"Toward the end it got a little scary," she said, "and I realized he had other intentions and I knew I was not where I should be. I just didn't quite know how to get myself out of there."

Years later, she recalled her discomfort after Polanski asked her to lie down on a bed. "I said, 'No, no. I don't want to go in there. No, I don't want to do this. No!' . . . We were alone and I didn't know what else would happen if I made a scene. So I was just scared, and after giving some resistance, I figured well, I guess I'll get to come home after this." Polanski performed oral, vaginal, and anal sex acts on the girl, still in the ninth grade. Like a true gentlemen, while Polanski was raping her, he asked Geimer if she was on birth control.

After Geimer informed the authorities of Polanski's assault, the director was arrested and pleaded guilty to unlawful sex with a minor, but before his sentencing, Polanski fled to London and later Paris to avoid prison. Once he was safely in Europe, Polanski made clear that he had little if any regret over his crime. "If I had killed somebody, it wouldn't have had so much appeal to the press, you see? But," he said, "f—ing, you see, and the young girls. Judges want to f— young girls. Juries want to f— young girls. Everyone wants to f— young girls!"

Even more remarkable than his rape was what happened in the decades that followed. Hollywood protected him and turned *him* into the victim. Petitions for him were launched by major Hollywood names like Martin Scorsese and accused child rapist Woody Allen. In 1979, he was nominated for an Oscar, and in 2002, he actually won the Academy Award for best director, which he could not accept in person to avoid arrest and prison time.

In short, because Polanski (like Woody Allen) was a notorious liberal—his 2010 film, *The Ghost Writer*, depicted a British prime minister, loosely based on Tony Blair, as a tool of a bizarre conspiracy orchestrated by a loosely fictionalized Bush administration and the ever-evil Halliburton—he is allowed to rape anyone he wants. But then, why should Hollywood treat its own any different than the other alleged rapists, deadbeat dads, and sexual abusers they've given millions to—from the Kennedys to John Edwards to Bill Clinton.

Hollywood's leading men were not the only people defending Polanski. Arch-liberal Whoopi Goldberg excused the incident. "I know it wasn't rape-rape," she said on *The View* in 2009. "It was something else, but I don't believe it was rape-rape." This from one of the vultures of *The View* who love to swoop in to attack Republicans for even using the word "rape" in an election. Further, when Woody Allen's adopted daughter Dylan Farrow wrote an open letter in the *New York Times* accusing Allen of raping her as a seven-year-old child, Hollywood stood by and watched.

"Woody Allen was never convicted of any crime. That he got away with what he did to me haunted me as I grew up. I was stricken with guilt that I had allowed him to be near other little girls. I was terrified of being touched by men. I developed an eating disorder. I began cutting myself. That torment was made worse by Hollywood. All but a precious few (my heroes) turned a blind eye. Most found it easier to accept the ambiguity, to say, 'Who can say what happened,' to pretend that nothing was wrong. Actors praised him at awards shows. Networks put him on TV. Critics put him in magazines. Each time I saw my abuser's face—on a poster, on a T-shirt, on television—I could only hide my panic until I found a place to be alone and fall apart," Farrow wrote in early 2014. "Last week, Woody Allen was nominated for his latest Oscar. But this time, I refuse to fall apart. For so long, Woody Allen's acceptance silenced me. It felt like a personal rebuke, like the awards and accolades were a way to tell me to shut up and go away. But the survivors of sexual abuse who have reached out to me—to support me and to share their fears of coming forward, of being called a liar, of being told their memories aren't their memories—have given me a reason to not be silent, if only so others know that they don't have to be silent either."

Allen denied the allegation. In 1997, Allen married his other adopted daughter, whom he started dating when she was just seventeen. He told *People* magazine in October 1976, "I'm open-minded about sex. I'm not above reproach; if anything, I'm below reproach. I mean, if I was caught in a love nest with fifteen twelve-year-old girls tomorrow, people would think, yeah, I always knew that about him." *The View*'s Barbara Walters defended him against Dylan Farrow's open letter and justified his preying on young girls.

"Supposedly she [Dylan] is very angry but she's doing it now because he's up for an award and so the question is, does your personal life interfere with the awards you may be getting?" Walters said.

Walters continued by arguing that the fact Allen likes young women has nothing to do with his work in Hollywood and said adopted children are not seen by their parents in the same way as biological children, justifying Allen's marriage to his adopted underage daughter.

Hollywood has never been short on hypocrisy—after all, look at the woman they made the prototype of the tough, independent woman: feminist icon Katharine Hepburn. As her Wikipedia entry puts it, "Hepburn came to epitomize the 'modern woman' in 20th-century America and is remembered as an important cultural figure."

Only in Hollywood would Hepburn be considered a "modern woman." An admitted adulterer, she slept her way through Hollywood's men and women. She once admitted, "I would have been a terrible mother, because I'm basically a very selfish human being." Hollywood's modern woman seemed to view men as something close to bizarre playthings. "I wouldn't give you ten men for any one woman," she once insisted. "All men are poops."

Katharine Hepburn was a talented actress and fascinating person with every right to consort with whom she chose. However, she is not the prototype of the average modern woman in America. Neither are the scores of sex-starved sirens posing as Hollywood's version of "the independent woman" today.

Hollywood: It's a place full of bright lights, pretty people, and golden opportunities. And from the outside looking in, it's a place where women can have it all: money, beauty, and fame. But the reality is Hollywood is a brutal and unforgiving city for women, where false expectations founder on a culture that chews up and spits out aspiring starlets, singers, and models.

Women in Hollywood are subjected to a constant string of humiliations, empty promises, and lies as they try to catch that "big break" that usually never comes. They're often forced to leave their families—and frequently their dignity—behind to become stars. It all sounds glamorous enough until they turn forty and realize all they've been doing for twenty years is serving coffee, waiting tables, and being turned down repeatedly by sexist casting directors and executives.

One thing makes Hollywood tick: Powerful men's interest in having sex with attractive women. "It's called f*ckability. 'I wanna f*ck her.' It's ordinary," actress Caroline Williams tells me. Williams, a horror-flick perennial (appearing in a number of the *Texas Chainsaw Massacre*, *Leprechaun*, and *Halloween* sequels), says, "It's an ordinary part of the language and it's talked about openly."

Although Williams has never experienced a situation in which she was asked to be involved with someone sexually in order to land a job in Tinseltown, she knows women who have been put into those positions by powerful people in a town that supposedly represents the culmination of decades of militant feminists redefining a more egalitarian, less "patriarchal" society.

"I'm absolutely aware of other stories women have told about various casting couch scenarios," says Williams. "You have to date somebody—'date' quote unquote. But women also, though, and this has to be noted, liberal women are frequently the very first to roll out the red carpet and make themselves available to anyone who will do anything for them. They understand that it's coin, that their beauty, accessibility, and availability is coin, and that's how they make their way through the process."

Williams points to 2013's critically acclaimed *Blue Is the Warmest Color* as an example. "This guy convinced these young girls to basically make a porn movie," she says, referring to director Abdellatif Kechiche. "It's high end. It's well lit. But that's what it is, and it won the Palme d'Or in Cannes," which is one of the most prestigious awards at the Cannes Film Festival.

Blue Is the Warmest Color features a young lesbian couple—the film starts with one of the duo at age fifteen—in numerous graphic sex scenes. Twenty minutes of the film are devoted to the two writhing and thrusting into each other, scenes that required hundreds of takes and screaming from the director as he made the actresses cry.

"He warned us that we had to trust him—blind trust—and give a lot of ourselves. He was making a movie about passion, so he wanted to have sex scenes, but without choreography—more like special sex scenes. He told us he didn't want to hide the characters' sexuality because it's an important part of every relationship," actress Adèle Exarchopoulos told the *Daily Beast*. "So he asked me if I was ready to make it, and I said, 'Yeah, of course!' because I'm young and pretty new to cinema. But once we were on the shoot, I realized that he really wanted us to give him everything. Most people don't even dare to ask the things that he did, and they're more respectful—you get reassured during sex scenes, and they're choreographed, which desexualizes the act."

"For us, it's very embarrassing," actress Léa Seydoux said about starring in the sex scenes for the film.

Seydoux and Exarchopoulos said they would never work with director Kechiche again.

Even *New York Times* film critic Manohla Dargis was stunned by the film's transparent use and abuse of two young actresses as sex objects: "In truth, it isn't sex per se that makes *Blue Is the Warmest Color* problematic; it's . . . the way it frames, with scrutinizing closeness, the female body."[1]

Another powerful Hollywood insider who would only speak to me on condition of anonymity described how studio executives and directors cast actresses in their films based on whom they are looking to sleep with. It's no wonder these are the same executives and directors who worship Bill Clinton and routinely shell out five-figure checks whenever he visits town for a political fundraiser; they act with the same abandon and disrespect toward women that he does.

Female executives, for their part, are forced to put up with the "I want to f*ck her so let's get her on the show" attitude of their male colleagues. If they don't, or if they speak up to their male bosses about vile comments and behavior, they'll never work another day in Hollywood.

"Women are sex objects. First and foremost in Hollywood, and for men, they're sex objects, that's just the way it is," actress Sam Sorbo, a longtime model and television actress (Serena on *Hercules*) tells me. "The whole construct is detrimental to young women and that's because Hollywood has bought into the feminist message which is detrimental to women. Hollywood has bought into this idea of basically free birth control, free abortion, free sex. For women, sex isn't free. For a woman the act comes with strings and they're trying to deny that, they're trying to get away from that. I don't think you can separate the two."

The pervasive sexism and view of women-as-sex-objects comes from a misogynistic view of women as tramps that is all around Hollywood. "Sexism is real and it persists in film and television. I've seen female directors openly undermined by male cinematographers in front of the entire crew. I've known female TV writers who've been fired for getting pregnant but were afraid to fight back lest they be blackballed," screenwriter, TV producer, and mom Liz Garcia wrote in *Forbes*.[2] "Female show runners [are] undermined by their agents in favor of male clients, even by the male writers they've hired. It goes on and on. It can be shockingly obvious. It goes unchecked. And honestly, to review all the examples makes me want to give up. And I can't."

Using actresses in films as porn stars isn't an isolated incident or a passing fad. The HBO series *Girls*, which has won multiple Emmys and Golden Globe awards, does the same thing. The show stars liberals' feminist hero of the moment, a gross and grotesque monstrosity named Lena Dunham.

The opening scene of the raunchy series begins by showing Hannah Horvath, a self-obsessed loser played by Dunham, at a low-lit dinner in New York City with her parents. During that dinner, her parents tell her it's time for them to cut her off financially. Horvath is stunned and tells her parents, "I can't believe you're doing this to me."

"We're not going to be supporting you any longer," her mother says.

"But I have no job," Hannah responds.

"No, you have an internship that you say is going to turn into a job," says her mother.

"I don't know when."

"You graduated from college two years ago. We've been supporting you for two years and that's enough."

"I'm your only child. It's not like I'm draining all of your resources, this feels very arbitrary," Dunham says, still stunned she would actually be asked by her parents to provide for herself as a twenty-four-year-old. Horvath, from Ohio, had been living off her parents in the most expensive city in the United States, New York, for years.

"We can't keep bankrolling your groovy lifestyle," her mother replies.

"My groovy lifestyle?"

"The bills add up, we're covering your rent, your insurance, your cell phone . . ."

"This is nuts . . . I am so close to the life I want . . ."

The conversation continues, with Hannah trying to guilt her parents into the idea that if they don't subsidize her life, she might turn into a drug-using, abortion-having wreck of a human being. To ease the shock of her parents' new policy, and after losing her internship because she doesn't have any real skills to offer the company in a full-time position, Hannah heads to the apartment of a guy named Adam, a dim bulb who repeatedly walks around half naked and whom she repeatedly uses for sexual gratification. Right before they have sex in what will be the first of many scenes in which Lena Dunham bares and flaunts it all, Adam tells her he hasn't applied for a job in a "long f*cking time." While they're having meaningless sex,

Dunham starts expressing a few concerns about what they're doing. He tells her, "Hey, let's play the quiet game." She complies.

The rest of *Girls* mostly involves more of Lena Dunham's self-indulgent pseudo-porn and uncomfortable scenes of one-night stands and liquor- and pill-fueled sex sessions that the show seems to makes the staple of any healthy twenty-something's life. Another scene features Dunham's character accompanying her friend to an abortion. "What was she going to do, have a baby and take it to her babysitting job? That's just unrealistic," she quips. When Hannah gets a full-time job, her male boss, who is just a "touchy kind of guy" who evokes San Diego mayor Bob Filner, sexually molests her. When she asks female colleagues what she should do about it, their response is, "You'll get used to it." Later, Hannah offers to sleep with her boss in order to get ahead in his company.

The second season of the show is equally revolting. It shows just as many pornographic sex scenes of Dunham and other female characters, portraying all young women as sex-crazed, unemployed, desperate losers—in other words, ideal Democratic base voters. The good news is that Adam actually cares about Hannah now. The bad news is that she's too busy sleeping with a married man.

I asked others in Hollywood about the show and whether it's a fair assessment of how the entertainment industry thinks of women. Caroline Williams said, "That's an accurate depiction of who Lena Dunham is. It may not be an accurate depiction of some of the other young girls that are in that show, but it's an accurate description of how *Sex and the City*, how they want to encourage young women to live, to take the brakes off, no restraint, no discipline. That's considered oppressive."

Girls is *Sex and the City* on steroids for a younger generation. It's even more pernicious, though, portraying women straight out of college as hopeless, broke, skill-less, nymphomaniac idiots. Say what you will about Sarah Jessica Parker's Carrie Bradshaw and the other main stars of the show—they at least had jobs or were financially independent in their own right. In *Girls*, there's a pervasive entitlement mentality that somehow, something is owed to young women who "just want to be who they are" in the most expensive city in the country.

"I'm going to have to, like, work at McDonald's," Hannah complains to another character. The other character points out that because Hannah is unemployed, working at McDonald's might be a good idea, but Hannah is having none of it. "It doesn't mean I [should] have to work there," she whines. "I went to college."

Liberal America rewards such nitwits with a TV series, a series of awards, and a multimillion-dollar book deal so she can spew this idiocy to any young woman who hasn't yet been despoiled by Hannah's vile and vulgar antics.

Consider also ABC's hit series, *Revenge*, which Hollywood billed as the story of two powerful women, played by Emily VanCamp and Madeleine Stowe, fighting for supremacy in the Hamptons. In reality, the two female leads portray women who betray their "true loves" on multiple occasions and use sex to manipulate men.

A ratings system adopted by Swedish Cinemas, known as the Bechdel test, takes a look at how women are portrayed in film. In order to pass the test, a film must accomplish three things:

1. It has to have at least two named women in it;
2. Those two named women must talk to each other; and
3. Those two named women must talk to each other about something other than a man.

A majority of major Hollywood films fail the Bechdel test. Most portray women as obsessed with men and their appearance. The not-so-subtle message is that women live frivolous lives outside of their pursuit of sexual satisfaction. "The entire *Lord of the Rings* trilogy, all *Star Wars* movies, *The Social Network*, *Pulp Fiction*, and all but one of the Harry Potter movies fail this test," Swedish art-house movie theater director Ellen Tejle told the *Guardian*[3] in 2013.

When the Bechdel test was applied to major 2013 films in the United States, the majority of them failed. Interestingly, *Iron Man 3* and *The Hunger Games: Catching Fire* passed. Both are movies with arguably conservative messages. In *Iron Man 3*, the hero battles terrorism and a villain with a more than passing resemblance to Osama bin Laden. *The Hunger Games* series is an obvious allegory about the perils of big government and brutal tyranny.

Bechdel isn't the only test that shows films portray women as desperate for male attention. Oxford Fellow Dr. Diane Purkiss has been pointing out for years that Hollywood increasingly portrays women as obsessed with men and their own physical appearance. "We really have reached a nadir in the way women are portrayed on screen. That is, I hope it is a nadir and doesn't sink further," Purkiss commented.[4] "Now, the only way for a woman to have a complex character on screen is to be depressing, tormented, and self-sacrificing." She points out that back in 1940s and 1950s Hollywood, big stars like Audrey Hepburn were given more substantial roles to play, instead of simply being put on screen as objects for men to ogle.

Further, a 2011 study[5] by Dr. Martha M. Lauzen, executive director of the Center for the Study of Women in Television and Film at San Diego State University, showed women are grossly underrepresented (although slowly increasing in representation) on the silver screen.

"In 2011, females remained dramatically under-represented as characters in film when compared with their representation of the U.S. population," Lauzen wrote about her findings. "Last year, females accounted for 33% of all characters in the top 100 domestic grossing films. This represents an increase of 5 percentage points since 2002 when females comprised 28% of characters."

Even as the number of female characters has increased, "The percentage of female protagonists has declined. In 2002, female characters accounted for 16% of protagonists. In 2011, females comprised only 11% of protagonists."

Lauzen also found female characters are significantly younger than their male counterparts in movies and are less likely to be portrayed as leaders. The majority of female characters are in their twenties and thirties, whereas the majority of male characters are in their thirties and forties. These numbers haven't changed since 2002.

"Overall, male characters account for 86% and females 14% of leaders. Broken down by type of leader, males comprise 93% of political and government leaders, 92% of religious leaders, 83% of business leaders, 73% of social leaders, and 70% of scientific and intellectual leaders."

Another study,[6] *Screening Sexy: Film Females and the Story That Isn't Changing*, produced in 2013 by the Annenberg School for Communication and Journalism at the University of Southern California, shows that out of the top one hundred films from 2012, with nearly forty-five hundred speaking characters, just 28.4 percent of characters were women, less than in previous years.

Across five years (2007, 2008, 2009, 2010 and 2012), 500 top-grossing films at the U.S. box office, and over 21,000 speaking characters, a new study by USC Annenberg found that females

represented less than one-third (28.4%) of all speaking characters in 2012 films. When they are on screen, 31% of women in
2012 were shown with at least some exposed skin, and 31.6%
were depicted wearing sexually revealing clothing.

Even worse? "There has been no meaningful change in the
prevalence of women on screen across the five years studied. In
fact, 2012 features the lowest percentage of females in the five
years covered in this report," said Communication Professor
Stacy L. Smith, the principal investigator. "The last few years
have seen a wealth of great advocacy for more women on screen.
Unfortunately, that investment has not yet paid off with an increase in female characters or a decrease in their hypersexualization."

The authors also examined how the presentation of women
varied by the age of the character. "The findings are as provoca-
tive as the outfits, especially when teenage female characters are
considered," Smith said.

Over half of female teen characters (56.6%) were shown in
sexy attire in 2012, compared with 39.9% of women between
the ages of 21 and 39. 2012 capped off a three-year increase
in the hypersexualization of teen girls, while for other age groups
the numbers do not show the same hike.

So why are more women being portrayed as desperate idiots in Hollywood films? A look at who's directing might help answer this question.

According to the Center for the Study of Women in Television
and Film at San Diego State University, only 7 percent of the directors of the past four years' top 250 films were women. According to
data collected by Fandor,[7] just 4.4 percent of directors for the top one

hundred box office films are women. The total number of female directors in Hollywood was down to just 5 percent in 2011 after being as high as 9 percent in 1998 and 7 percent in 2010.

In nearly a century, only four female directors have even been *nominated* for an Oscar, and it wasn't until 2010 that a female director finally won. When Kathryn Bigelow took home an Academy Award, at the age of fifty-eight, for her film *The Hurt Locker*, Bigelow said it was the most incredible moment of her life. It speaks volumes about Hollywood that Bigelow is the only woman who has ever had that moment.

"There've been a lot of studies done on this, and I think the primary reason why women directors feel stalled in their careers is they feel that the doors to financing are closed to them," said Mynette Louie, president of Gamechanger Films, a new company focusing on getting more women into Hollywood directing.[8] "Most of the decision makers, when it comes to financing, are men. So I think there is this gender bias, whether spoken or unspoken, that's sort of there underlying that financing structure."

"They [directors] make movies for their friends," Hollywood actress Caroline Williams told me about directors in the industry. She explained that directors make films that portray how they think about certain topics or feel about certain groups of people. "Increasingly they make smaller, more politically directed films where they can pat one another on the back and celebrate themselves."

One bright spot for the industry lies in the horror genre, of all places, where Williams made her mark. In horror, women are often given lead character roles. Unsurprisingly, much of the genre is produced and directed outside the Hollywood elite bubble.

"Because I am a genre actress, I do a lot of horror films. The typical horror fan is a man or woman who is between New York and

LA, and they tend to come from more religious backgrounds. They have a well-defined idea of what good and bad are, wrong and right. They have a strong moral sensibility, and it's an entirely different world when I travel to those states doing conventions and things like that," Williams says. "In LA, the horror film genre is looked down on primarily I think for that reason, because you're making a product that appeals to other people than them. And increasingly the way they like to see women is through the political prism that they enjoy looking through and increasingly as you watch their products, it's not the broad audience films like *The Hunger Games*, which is clearly now making a very strong statement as far as I'm concerned toward people of our political persuasion."

To make things worse, women in liberal Hollywood are still well behind men in terms of guild membership and pay for acting and writing. This isn't because women aren't choosing to go into these fields, but because Hollywood men's clubs keep them out. Major acting and directing guilds are headed by men. And most of those numbers haven't budged in recent years.

"One lonely area where the gap has narrowed, according to the Writers Guild of America West, is in the median pay for writing in film," the *Hollywood Reporter* reported[9] in 2011. "But that's because men's earnings are dropping while women are holding their ground or improving ever-so-slightly. Even so, the guys retain an edge: In 2009, the median annual pay in film was about $76,500 for men, compared with $62,500 for women. (Men did better in television that year, too, though the gap was narrower: $108,000 on average for men, as opposed to $98,600 for women.)"

Women also have fewer years to earn money in Hollywood. Their career lifespans are much shorter than those of men in the same positions. "It's been a male-dominated business since the beginning of time," Gail Berman told *The Hollywood Reporter*.[10] "It hasn't changed all that much."

"There is quite a lot of denial regarding this issue in the business," diversity coordinator for the Writers Guild of America West Kim Meyers added.[11] "I haven't heard a lot of serious conversation about it."

When I talked to radio host and actress Shemane Nugent about this persistent problem, she described a "man's world" with few doors open to women. "There's really no doors that are open at all and especially if you don't have any connections," she said. "It's almost like you have to be in the boys' gang before you can really play the game, and I'm never going to be there so it's really been a struggle for me."

Nugent's work has received good reviews from William Morris, one of the country's largest talent agencies, but that hasn't been enough. "Yeah, I get good reviews, but then where does that get me?" she asks. "I have to know a producer or something to get the screenplay made into a film."

Ironically, the same women who work in what feminists would describe as a system dominated by "patriarchy" aren't interested in helping women get ahead, unless of course those women agree with the Hollywood elite that America is a terrible country. They want women who agree with Sean Penn when he says, "I was brought up in a country that relished fear-based religion, corrupt government, and an entire white population living on stolen property that they murdered for and that is passed on from generation to generation." They want women like Janeane Garofalo, who said, "Our country is founded on a sham: Our forefathers were slave-owning rich white guys who wanted it their way. So when I see the American flag, I go, 'Oh, my God, you're insulting me.'" And they want women like Jane

Fonda, who flew to Hanoi to support the North Vietnamese soldiers killing American troops and who posed for a picture sitting behind an anti-aircraft gun used to shoot down American planes.

Shemane Nugent has refused to buy into Hollywood's received liberal wisdom, and she's paid a price for it. "One time I sat down with a production company, two women, in Los Angeles who wanted to produce one of my screenplays," Nugent said, adding that her husband, Ted Nugent, was traveling the same day, so she kept her phone on in case of an emergency. "It was a lunch and it was casual and we had other friendly conversation, and Ted had called me and I excused myself and answered the phone. We talked for maybe thirty seconds and I said you know, 'Gosh I'm really sorry I took that I just wanted to make sure my husband was okay, he played the Star Spangled Banner at a Glenn Beck rally with Sarah Palin.' And then for a split second I caught the looks on their faces, like, it was suddenly, it turned from a friendly gaze to a cold stare and there was one of those awkward pauses, and one of the women said, 'I guess that means you're a Sarah Palin fan.'"

Before responding, Nugent ran a few different scenarios through her head. She had worked really hard on this screenplay and wanted to get it produced, but didn't want to be dishonest.

"Yeah," she told me, "I thought about, shoot, should I lie to them? Should I cover it? I have worked my butt off writing this screenplay—I mean it's like another marriage when you put your heart and soul into a project, it takes years. And so I paused for a second, I ran all those thoughts through my mind and I answered, 'Yes, as a matter of fact I am,'" she said.

The conversation about her screenplay was over.

"Well, I guess we'll just leave it at that," one of the women said, and they left the lunch.

"There is a stigma and it is unfortunate. It isn't just me that it happens to, it happens to a lot of conservatives." Nugent says. "We are all afraid to speak our minds and talk about who we support. It makes you feel like there's a blemish or that it's dishonoring to be a conservative in Hollywood, which is why I think people are trying to produce films outside of Hollywood."

Nugent isn't alone. Actress Maria Conchita Alonso, who starred in *Moscow on the Hudson* with Robin Williams, was recently booted from a San Francisco production of *The Vagina Monologues* after endorsing a Tea Party assemblyman for his anti-illegal-immigration stance. Major actresses like Melissa Joan Hart, Stacey Dash, and Patricia Heaton have received vicious attacks for openly supporting Republican candidates and conservative political views.

Meanwhile Obama lover Bill Cosby, previously best known for wearing hideous sweaters, gets virtually a free pass for the alleged groping and possible assault of women (for which he has not been found guilty and presumably denies all allegations), including an accuser who was nineteen years old. Here's what she told *Newsweek* in an article posted on February 7, 2014:

[Bill Cosby] asked me to help him raise capital for a club he wanted to start. One day, I called him to cancel a meeting because I was feeling really sick, and he said, "Why don't you come over to this restaurant I'm at, you'll feel better if you have lunch." I sat down, and he gave me what he said was two pills of [an over-the-counter cold medicine]. I swallowed them, and 20 minutes later I felt terrific; 30 minutes later, I was face-down in my soup. He volunteered to take me home. And then, because I was so ill, he volunteered to undress me and put me to bed. I started fighting him—I took a lamp and broke a window. He finally left.

When I woke up, I saw that he left two 100-dollar bills on the table next to my front door. I was so sincerely and deeply infuriated that, even through the drugs.... I was crazed. I wanted to rip his neck off. The next day, I went to go visit my brother, who was in the terminal ward at a children's hospital. Cosby, smart man that he is, had been to the hospital to give presents to the kids. By the time I got to the hospital, my brother was glowing that the great Bill Cosby had given him a portable radio.

Cosby continues to praise Democrats like Obama and compare Republicans to segregationists, as he did in March 2013 when he said that Republicans who didn't applaud Obama's State of the Union address were "as bad as the people who were against any kind of desegregation."

So, too, David Letterman was absolved of a string of affairs and a confession of adultery in an interview with Oprah Winfrey. His loathsome behavior is excused, of course, as long as he attacks Sarah Palin on television and admits, as he did to radio host Howard Stern, that he's never voted for a Republican in his life. Letterman, whose reckless behavior left him the victim of an extortion plot, even had the nerve to called George W. Bush "a stooge" for *his* behavior with women, citing a harmless backrub Bush once gave to German Chancellor Angela Merkel. "He doesn't know any better," Letterman said of Bush. In other words, those Republicans just don't know how to treat their women.

The former star of *Clarissa Explains It All* and *Sabrina the Teenage Witch* Hart tweeted in 2012 that she was voting for Mitt Romney. In response, she was called, in her words, "every name in the book." Haters said they hoped she would die and that they hoped her children are gay, "which was like somehow supposed to be some sort of punishment." She added that the "hate was really unbelievable." [12]

When *Clueless* actress Stacey Dash expressed her support for Romney in 2012, after voting for Obama in 2008, she was told to go "kill herself" and accused of "betraying her race."

Then, again, it could have been worse for Dash. At least she wasn't forced to sleep with a creepy casting director in order to get a role, required to film a porn scene in *Blue Is the Warmest Color*, or anally raped in the ninth grade by Roman Polanski.

For women in "liberal" Tinseltown, misfortune is relative.

CHAPTER 11

THE NRA: AMERICA'S REAL PRO-WOMEN'S GROUP

And you don't know if you feel like you're gonna be raped, or if you feel like someone's been following you around or if you feel like you're in trouble and when you may actually not be, that you pop out that gun and you pop—pop a round at somebody.

—*State Representative Joe Salazar (D-Colo.)*

Before women had a right to vote, they had a right to own a firearm. God may have made man and woman, but as the old saying goes, Sam Colt made them equal.

Sure, birth control pills are great, but they don't come in handy during a fight against a guy who is trying to kill you. It will forever boggle my mind that rabid feminist groups aren't telling their members to learn how to use and carry a handgun. These are the same groups who scream about equality between men and women, yet dismiss one of the greatest equalizers of all.

It's not just feminist groups that miss the boat on the link between gun rights and gender equality. It's also the Democratic Party.

If Democratic politicians cared about women's equality as much as they say, they would be the nation's biggest champions of gun rights. Nancy Pelosi would have a perfect 100 percent voting record with the National Rifle Association. Hillary Clinton would be stumping for pro-gun candidates. Barack Obama would be playing golf with Wayne LaPierre.

Every six minutes in America, there is a forcible rape. That's three hundred thousand women violently raped every single year, and according to the Department of Justice, that's a low estimate. The CDC guesses that as many as 1.5 million women are raped every year.

What is a woman's best defense against sexual assault? A gun. Nearly three hundred thousand women use handguns every year to defend themselves against a sexual assault. Unfortunately, Democratic politicians want to make it harder to own a gun—and harder for women to protect themselves.

Unfortunately, British women have learned the hard way the relationship between gun rights and protection from sexual assault. Guns are much more difficult to obtain in Britain, and according to research conducted and published by David Kopel, a professor of constitutional law at Denver University and a policy analyst at the Cato Institute,[1] a "woman in Great Britain is three times more likely to be raped than an American woman."

Often anti-gun advocates point to Great Britain as a shining example of how gun control works, but when it comes to violent crime—homicide, rape, robbery, and aggravated assault—England and Wales have a higher rate than the United States. Scotland, Western Europe's most violent nation and Britain's murder capital, is even worse. The government officials in that violent country have strict gun control and bans on carrying knives, yet knives are used in half of the homicides each year. People living in Scotland have a nearly one-in-five chance of being a victim of assault, according to government statistics.

British women are also more likely to be burglarized while they're home. "In the United States, only about 13 percent of home burglaries take place when the occupants are home," says Kopel, "but in Great Britain, about 59 percent do. American burglars report that they avoid occupied homes because of the risk of getting shot. English burglars prefer occupied homes, because there will be wallets and purses with cash, which does not have to be fenced at a discount."

Despite the evidence of gun control in Britain leading to more violence against women, American Democrats like Barack Obama continue to insist that gun control means crime control. He was in for an unpleasant surprise, however, when he ordered the Centers for Disease Control and Prevention to study gun violence in America. A few months and $10 million later, the CDC came back with predictable results: People who are armed or who are likely to be armed are far less likely to be attacked or harmed by a criminal. This means less rape and assault on armed women.

The report found "studies that directly assessed the effect of actual defensive uses of guns (i.e., incidents in which a gun was 'used' by the crime victim in the sense of attacking or threatening an offender) have found consistently lower injury rates among gun-using crime victims compared with victims who used other self-protective strategies."

Those "other self-protective strategies" that have been proven to be less effective in preventing injuries and harm to innocent victims are exactly the kinds of strategies the Democratic Party and its liberal, anti-gun crusaders have been advocating for years.

Take for example the Brady Law. In 1993, President Bill Clinton signed legislation that required a five-day waiting period for firearms purchases. Scholar and economist John Lott found through his research that after the Brady bill became law, the country saw a 3 percent jump in rapes and violent assaults against women. If only Democrats in Congress had paid more attention to the effects of state-law waiting periods in the years before the Brady Law, they might have realized that the legislation wasn't the crime-prevention silver bullet its sponsors promised it would be.

One of the women affected by a state-law waiting period was Bonnie Elmasri. In 1991, Elmasri and her two children were murdered in cold blood by her husband. Just one day before the crime, Elmasri made a phone call inquiring about how to purchase a handgun, mentioning her husband had been making violent threats against her and her children. The answer she received cost her and her children their lives: Wisconsin had a two-day waiting period for handgun purchases.

An article in the *Pittsburg Post-Gazette*[2] from April, 6, 1991, told the story of a woman who faced a similar problem:

Last year, a mail carrier named Catherine Latta of Charlotte, N.C., went to the police to obtain permission to buy a handgun. Her ex-boyfriend had previously robbed her, assaulted her several times and raped her.

The clerk at the sheriff's office informed her the gun permit would take two to four weeks. "I told her I'd be dead by then," Ms. Latta later recalled.

That afternoon, she went to a bad part of town and bought an illegal $20 semiautomatic pistol on the street. Five hours later, her ex-boyfriend attacked her outside her house, and she shot him dead. The county prosecutor decided not to prosecute Ms. Latta for either the self-defense homicide or the illegal gun.

Fast-forward to the Colorado State Legislature's debate in 2013, when Democrats suggested women could rely on bodily functions and call boxes, not a gun, to save them from rape.

During debate about legislation eliminating concealed carry on college campuses, Colorado Democratic Representative Joe Salazar argued that call boxes and whistles were sufficient to protect women from rape. "There are some gender inequities on college campuses, this is true and universities have been faced with that situation for a long time," he observed. "It's why we have call boxes, it's why we have safe zones, that's why we have the whistles. Because you just don't know who you're gonna be shooting at. And you don't know if you feel like you're gonna be raped, or if you feel like someone's been following you around or if you feel like you're in trouble and when you may actually not be, that you pop out that gun and you pop—pop a round at somebody."

That's right ladies, this Democratic man knows better than you when it comes to how you feel about maybe getting raped. You don't really know how you feel about that creep following you home after class. But don't worry. You're in a "safe zone." A call box will save you.

Although feminist organizations claim to stand up for rape victims, they were silent on his comments about women not really knowing if they are going to get raped.[3] Salazar got a free pass for his inanity for two reasons: Feminist groups like Democrats, and they dislike guns.

Like Representative Salazar, the University of Colorado–

Colorado Springs advises women to avoid rape with tactics that are far less effective than a gun—like puking and peeing. It's the triple *P*: puking, peeing, and pens. If that doesn't work, the suggestion is to passively resist, or, in other words, let it happen.

What to Do if You Are Attacked

These tips are designed to help you protect yourself on campus, in town, at your home, or while you travel. These are preventative tips and are designed to instruct you in crime prevention tactics.

- Be realistic about your ability to protect yourself.
- Your instinct may be to scream, go ahead! It may startle your attacker and give you an opportunity to run away.
- Kick off your shoes if you have time and can't run in them.
- Don't take time to look back; just get away.
- If your life is in danger, passive resistance may be your best defense.
- Tell your attacker that you have a disease or are menstruating.
- Vomiting or urinating may also convince the attacker to leave you alone.
- Yelling, hitting or biting may give you a chance to escape, do it!
- Understand that some actions on your part might lead to more harm.
- Remember, every emergency situation is different. Only you can decide which action is most appropriate.

Contrary to university bureaucrats' beliefs, the "most appropriate" action will sometimes be pulling out a .38 Special and making sure that your rapist never attacks another woman again. No bodily functions necessary, only a steady hand.

If you're thinking that college campuses tend to be safe places for young women, think again. When the address of any major college is inserted into a local sex offender registry, dozens of addresses where convicted offenders are living pop up. For example, George Washington University in Washington, D.C., is within a half-mile of nineteen convicted sex offenders.[4] Just outside of the University of Arizona are more than two dozen convicted sex offenders. It's the same story outside the University of Southern California.

Unfortunately, many universities have anti-gun policies that make it easier for nearby sexual predators to prey on innocent college girls—like the University of Nevada–Reno's Amanda Collins.

It was ten o'clock on a fall evening in 2007, and Amanda Collins had just finished taking a midterm. After the test, she left the classroom with a group of friends to walk back to a nearby parking garage. Amanda could have parked across campus, but figured it was safer at night not to walk so far in the dark.

"The conversation was normal conversation from a bunch of college students who had just taken an exam," Amanda said. " 'Oh, my gosh, what did you put down for this question?' or you know, 'Oh, I couldn't remember this,' 'What do you think she [professor] was after?' "

When the group reached the parking garage, Amanda broke off to get her car on the ground floor of the complex. Growing up, her parents taught her to be aware of her surroundings at all times, to pay attention, and to be alert. They also insisted she have martial arts training and required her to obtain a second-degree black belt before receiving her driver's license.

"I surveyed the area but it was pretty desolate because it was ten o'clock at night, and seeing no threat under my vehicle or around me,

I wished the group well, and they went up, and I continued to walk to my vehicle at an angle, everything I was doing was second nature. I didn't have to think about it just because it was so ingrained in me growing up."

But Amanda wasn't alone in that parking garage. A man named James Biela was hiding behind the wheel well of a truck, waiting.

"He grabbed me from behind, forced me to the ground, and once I was on the ground he put a pistol to my temple, clicked off the safety, told me not to say anything, and then he brutally raped me. While he was raping me, I could see the university police cruisers parked because that was the floor that they parked the cruisers on, and their offices had closed for the night ... so I knew, I knew, that no one was coming for me. That there was just no help coming. I later found out that I was less than one hundred feet away from their office."

Amanda had a concealed carry permit with her that night, but she didn't have her gun, because the University of Nevada–Reno was a "gun-free zone." Of course, making a college a "gun-free zone" doesn't mean it's free of guns. Amanda was raped at gunpoint in a gun-free zone.

Amanda didn't decide to report the crime, she went into survival mode and tried to forget about the incident, until she heard of a young woman, Brianna Denison, who had gone missing:

A sophomore psychology student at Santa Barbara City College, she had returned to her Reno, Nev., home for winter break and planned to attend a number of events associated with the SWAT 72 snowboarding festival on Saturday night, January 19, 2008, before heading back to college the next week. She made a list of the events she was planning to attend, gave it to her mother and informed her that she would be ending the night at the home of a friend, K. T. Hunter, also 19. . . .

After they changed into sleeping attire, Hunter gave Denison two blankets, a pillow and a teddy bear to bolster the pillow.

Denison slept on the leather sofa downstairs, while Hunter retired to her bedroom that she shared with another girl. She took her dog with her and locked the bedroom door behind her. The five-foot, ninety-eight-pound Denison presumably went to sleep on the sofa, in view of a glass-paneled front door that was left unlocked, as Hunter and the other girls living in the house typically left their doors. When Hunter awoke some five hours later and began looking for her friend, all she found was a silver-dollar-sized bloodstain on the pillow that investigators would later determine had come from Denison.[5]

Brianna's body was found in a snowy field on February 16, 2008. She was raped and strangled to death by the same man who raped Amanda Collins and a third woman.

Collins has no doubt it was her university's "gun-free" policies that made those tragedies possible. "If I had been carrying that night, two other rapes could have been prevented and a young life would have been saved," Collins said.[6]

After Denison's rape, university officials told Amanda she could carry her firearm so long as she didn't tell anyone about it, and if she did, her right to carry would immediately be revoked.

Democrats have a gross disdain for women like Collins who want to protect themselves through their Second Amendment rights. When Gayle Trotter, a mother and senior fellow at the Independent Women's Forum, testified in favor of women's gun rights before Congress in 2013, dozens of anti-gun activists in the back of the room made it a point to bully and intimidate Trotter every time she opened her mouth to answer a question. Trotter was loudly heckled after she suggested women need firearms to protect young children in their homes.

"An assault weapon in the hands of a young woman defending her babies at her home becomes a defense weapon," Trotter said as jeers erupted. "Guns are the great equalizer during a violent confrontation."

My cousin Tiffany learned what an equalizer guns can be after a convicted felon began stalking her. He would show up out of the blue at Tiffany's house and would call her whenever he pleased. Tiffany was especially frightened when her husband, Mark, left her with her two kids while he traveled overseas for work. Finally, Tiffany and Mark bought some guns for the home, and she says, "I feel safer at home when Mark is gone and I feel empowered to protect myself and my kids, especially if my stalker friend were to stop by and try something. I would recommend owning a gun for protection to any woman who may fear being alone at home. It is your constitutional right."

Like Tiffany, Julie Temple was hesitant about having a gun in her home or purse, but when a man accosted her and her toddler son while she was shopping, a veteran with a concealed carry license rescued them. After that, she asked her husband for shooting lessons, and after some initial nervousness, she learned to shoot with accuracy, calmness, and confidence. She says, "I have shot almost every gun in my husband's collection. I can load them, clean them, and I love that I don't feel scared of them anymore. I was so fearful of them I wouldn't even touch one, let my kids touch them. My husband took my son hunting and I cried out of fear because I thought guns were the bad part of the equation. Now I go target shooting with him and our son. My daughter will learn, too, now that she's eight." Julie was a Democrat who voted for Obama before her midlife conversion on gun rights. Now she's a registered Republican and a proud member of the NRA.

Tiffany and Julie are far from the only women who were once afraid of guns but now realize that, contrary to what the Democratic Party is always saying, gun ownership is an important way for women to protect themselves. In the spring of 2013, one of *The View*'s liberal co-hosts, Sherri Shephard, explained what had changed her mind about owning a gun.

"At one in the morning the alarm in our house went off," recounted Shephard. The alarm sounded, "Warning, intruder! Get out of the house! It scared me so bad." When her husband, Sal, went downstairs to look around the house, Shephard realized there was nothing upstairs to protect her and her son Jeffrey, who was asking, "Mommy, what's wrong?" She says:

> I'm trying to calm Jeffrey down and all I had was this wicker basket, that's all I had was this wicker basket because you mess with Jeffrey, all I had was a wicker garbage can and I said, "We have nothing, Sal doesn't . . . we don't have a bat, nothing. We're going to get a gun." I told Sal, because you know, you've got my child in here and my husband was down there trying to protect the home, and it just made me realize how vulnerable you are if you can't protect your home. And the police are wonderful, they came about seven minutes later, but to me, that's seven minutes too late.

Luckily for Sherri and her family, the incident was only a false alarm.

•   •   •

If the Democratic Party has its way, women like Amanda Collins will never be able to protect themselves with a gun in a college parking lot. Women like Tiffany, Julie, and Sherri Shephard will be left to the "most appropriate" defenses of "vomiting or urinating" when attacked. And the police will always arrive "seven minutes too late."

BATTERED VOTER SYNDROME

There is not the woman born who desires to eat the bread of dependence, no matter whether it be from the hand of father, husband, or brother; for any one who does so eat her bread places herself in the power of the person from whom she takes it.

—*Susan B. Anthony*

It is an age-old question: Why are so many good women drawn to such disastrous men? Liars, manipulators, and sleazebags who abuse them, lie to them, even brainwash them just to have their way. That's how the Democrats have been seducing women for decades—and Republicans have let them get away with it. The GOP has played the role of the long-suffering friend watching one woman after another fall for the same jerks again and again.

How long before the Republicans realize that they don't have to be on the losing side of the media-created "war on women?"

Yes, Republicans do have a problem with women. The problem is not that women are incapable of supporting conservatives—Ronald

Reagan was able to take home a whopping twelve-point margin of victory among women in 1984 despite his opponent Walter Mondale choosing Geraldine Ferraro as his running mate with the support of the National Organization for Women. The problem is that Republicans have fallen for the media-driven spin that their issues don't relate to female voters.

American women are being "othered" by the Democrats. As with African-Americans and Hispanics and Jews, we are being carved out of the political process as just another special interest group that Big Government must pander to. Women are told that they couldn't, or shouldn't, possibly care about such issues as tax relief, a strong defense, restrained federal spending—you know, *men* issues. Instead, the interests of women voters have been redefined as unlimited birth control, wanton sex, and free abortions. Almost every Democratic campaign commercial in the last few election cycles geared toward women has focused on one or all of these issues. The subtext is that women are either too immoral or too stupid to avoid sleeping around and getting pregnant. That it is now government's responsibility to protect us from ourselves. We've been brainwashed into thinking that there is such a thing as "women's issues" to begin with. If Republicans don't fight back, women are going to be as solid a voting bloc for Democrats as other special-interest groups who have become convinced they are dependent on Washington bureaucrats in order to safeguard their "rights."

Why is it, by the way, that when Republicans lose the women's vote, as they did in 2012, they have a serious problem with female voters, but when Al Gore and John Kerry lose the male vote, as they did in 2000 and 2004, and as Obama did in 2012, there's no problem at all? Why don't the media ask why Democrats are waging a war on men? They won't because the point of this "war on women" rhetoric isn't really to improve the lives of women. It's to help the Democrats win elections by manipulating female voters.

And why not? It's working. More than 54 percent of the electorate in 2012 was composed of women, and Obama carried the women's vote by a staggering eleven points. The robust double-X-chromosome vote was enough to tilt key swing states such as Ohio, New Hampshire, and Florida in Obama's favor. Had there been no rhetoric about the "war on women" and no fear tactics about the coming GOP bogeyman armed with forceps in one hand and a trans-vaginal ultrasound in the other, Barack Obama would almost certainly be back in Hawaii, playing even more golf than he does already.

The "they're coming for my birth control" meme has been used with devastating effectiveness by liberals. And it may be what keeps the White House in Democratic hands for the foreseeable future, especially if the Benedict Arnold of the women's rights movement, Hillary "look the other way" Clinton, does the expected and runs for president in 2016.

It shouldn't be this easy for them. Just look at the crowd of creeps and liars who lead the Democratic Party today.

I'm not just talking about Bill Clinton, the alleged rapist whose wife used her husband's embarrassing pattern of sexual misconduct and assault to get people to feel sorry for her and thus launch her own political career.

Nor am I referring only to that notorious House of Horndogs more commonly known as the sainted Kennedy family, who seem never to have found a woman they couldn't demean, cheat on, or lobotomize. That's just the tip of the iceberg. How about the slew of would-be presidents from Gary Hart to John "Who's Your Daddy?" Edwards to Bill Richardson to Al Gore?

And let's not forget would-be mayors like Clinton protégé Anthony Weiner.

To paraphrase Michael Douglas in *The American President*, how can the Democratic Party defend people who claim to love women but clearly can't stand the women they're married to? And why do the rest of us sit around and say nothing? Republicans do have candidates from time to time who stupidly opine about rape. But the Democrats have leaders who are actually accused of it, then go on to be praised by "women's groups" and win re-election.

If Republicans want to win and promote a sound pro-life, pro-women agenda, then it is time that they learn to play hardball in the same way that the Democrats do. The only difference is that the GOP doesn't need to lie, exaggerate, and frighten in order to win back women as a voting bloc. If Republicans are waging a war on women, then the male Democratic elite is waging a war on the truth.

Which party consistently voted against securing fundamental and equal rights for American women? The Democratic Party, of course. This is not a trick question, just one that has been manipulated and obscured for years now at the expense of endless inept Republicans. You might think that the party that loves resurrecting male leaders from its past—Lincoln, Teddy Roosevelt, Reagan—would proudly raise up the first ever female congresswoman, Jeannette Rankin, a Republican from Wyoming. When faced with attacks for opposing "women's rights," how about reminding the American public of the grand coalition between suffragettes and the Republican Party to push woman's suffrage in the face of Woodrow Wilson and the Democratic Congress's fierce opposition. When the Nineteenth Amendment finally broke through the Democratic-controlled house, the final tally in the Senate was thirty-six Republicans for, eight against, and twenty Democrats for, seventeen against. The amendment was then sent to the states. The trend was resoundingly the same. Twenty-six of the thirty-six states that ratified the Nineteenth Amendment had Republican legislatures. Of the nine states that voted against ratification, eight were Democratic.

If Republicans simply put the question to their opponents, "Have you changed since your party sought to keep women from voting?" they would at least be on the offensive for once. If they were even more fluent than just that in exposing the real "war on women" by the Democratic elite, they would be winning elections.

As a single woman covering political campaigns, I've noticed that the tactics used to woo female voters are very similar to those used in the dating world. Liberal Democrats pull up in a shiny car. They offer some false compliments. They try to impress by throwing around lots of cash. They lie to you and tell you they are interested in you, but really they're interested in using you before they move on to the next woman. They bank on your thinking with what's between your legs instead of what's in your head. In the end, liberals end up driving off with another girl in the shiny car they can't really afford, whether it's Obamacare, free contraception for all, or other big government goodies that are bankrupting the country. Meanwhile, you're stuck with the dinner bill.

Conservative Republicans offer the opposite. They aren't, generally speaking, sexy. They don't always have the fancy car. They save their money. They're practical. They appreciate women as individuals, not as replicated toys to play with or to show off in the front seat of their car. Democrats are the jocks who never grow up. Republicans are the steady responsible men you should be marrying.

When it comes to elections, women are being systematically played by the Democratic Party, and it's time that they really assert their independence by no longer being political pawns. That's why

I wrote this book. It exposes the true "war on women" that is being waged by the Democratic elite, using women for their own political benefit. This book will arm conservatives in the fight against this false and vitriolic broken-record alarmism over women's rights that obscures the real failures of the Democratic Party for all Americans. Finally, and most important, it will urge the GOP to go on the offensive, armed with data, real reporting, and the truth. It's about time.

We just need to wake up and realize that—to paraphrase Ronald Reagan—liberals, feminist groups, and the Democratic Party are not the solution to our problems. They *are* the problem!

NOTES

INTRODUCTION: THE C-WORD

1. Larry Flynt: Freedom fighter, pornographer, monster? by Johann Hari. May 27, 2011. http://www.independent.co.uk/news/people/profiles/larry-flynt-freedom-fighter-pornographer-monster-2289592.html.

2. Democratic Official Allan Brauer Wishes Death on Ted Cruz Aide's Children, by Washington Free Beacon Staff. September 20, 2013. http://freebeacon.com/politics/democratic-official-allan-brauer-wishes-death-on-ted-cruz-aides-children/.

3. Allan Brauer: CAUTION, LEFT WING LANGUAGE AHEAD, by Andrew Amedee. March 11, 2013. http://conservativereport.org/caution-democrat-language-ahead/.

4. Kentucky Progressive Group Tweets Racist Conspiracy About Mitch McConnell's Wife, by Evan McMorris-Santoro. February 26, 2013. http://talkingpointsmemo.com/dc/kentucky-progressive-group-tweets-racist-conspiracy-about-mitch-mcconnell-s-wife.

5. Report: Bill Maher doubles down—calls Sarah Palin the 'c' word, by Jeff Poor. March 29, 2011. http://dailycaller.com/2011/03/29/report-bill-maher-doubles-down-calls-sarah-palin-c-word/.

6. The Playboy Article (NSFW), by Caleb Howe. June 2, 2009. http://www.redstate.com/absentee/2009/06/02/the-playboy-article-nsfw/.

7. Laura Ingraham Busts *The View*: When Ed Schultz Called Me a Slut Barbara Walters 'Laughed It Off,' by Noel Sheppard. March 6, 2012. http://newsbusters.org/blogs/noel-sheppard/2012/03/06/laura-ingraham-busts-view-when-ed-schultz-called-me-slut-barbara-walt.

8. Olbermann: Without 'Fascistic Hatred,' Malkin Is Just a 'Mashed-Up Bag of Meat with Lipstick,' by Brad Wilmouth. October 13, 2009. http://www.newsbusters.org/blogs/brad-wilmouth/2009/10/13/olber mann-without-fascistic-hatred-malkin-just-mashed-bag-meat-lipsti.

9. The flames of hatred: 30 years of loathing for Baroness Thatcher explodes in celebrations of her death. Will funeral now be targeted? by James Chapman, Michael Seamark, Chris Greenwood, Lucy Os-borne and Jill Reilly. April 10, 2013. http://www.dailymail.co.uk/news /article-2306165/Margaret-Thatcher-death-parties-The-Lefts-sick -celebration-Brixtons-streets.html.

1: VAGINA VOTERS

1. Bye-Bye, Cooch, by Dahlia Lithwick. November 5, 2013. http:// www.slate.com/blogs/xx_factor/2013/11/05/ken_cuccinelli_loses_in_ virginia_women_say_no_thanks_we_re_cool.html.

2. I have been a member of the National Organization for Women since June 2013. In order to attend the annual NOW conference, you must be a member.

3. Turning to Fairness, by National Women's Law Center. March 2012. http://www.nwlc.org/sites/default/files/pdfs/nwlc_2012_turningto fairness_report.pdf.

4. Why Women (Like Me) Choose Lower-Paying Jobs, by Lisa Chow. September 11, 2013. http://www.npr.org/blogs/money/2013 /09/11/220748057/why-women-like-me-choose-lower-paying-jobs.

5. An Analysis of Reasons for the Disparity in Wages Between Men and Women, by CONSAD Research Corp. for the U.S. Dept. of Labor. January 12, 2009. http://www.consad.com/content/reports /Gender%20Wage%20Gap%20Final%20Report.pdf.

6. Party Line: The Most Powerful Call In Politics, by CBS News. January 27, 2009. http://www.cbsnews.com/news/party-line-the-most -powerful-call-in-politics/.

2: LYNCHING THE GOP

1. *Inside the White House*, by Ronald Kessler. (Simon & Schuster, Au-gust 2, 1995).

3: RISE OF THE FEMI-MARXIST

1. Human Poverty in Transition Economies: Regional Overview for HDR 1997, by Ewa Ruminska-Zimny. http://hdr.undp.org/sites /default/files/ewa_ruminska.pdf.

2. Single mothers, poverty and depression, by George W. Brown and Patricia M. Moran. *Psychological Medicine* 27 (1997), pp. 21–33.

3. *The Feminine Mystique*, by Betty Friedan (Dell mass market paperback edition, 1964), p. 85.

4. *It Changed My Life: Writings on the Women's Movement*, by Betty Friedan (Harvard University Press, 1998).

5. Marriage: America's Greatest Weapon Against Child Poverty, by Robert Rector. September 5, 2012. http://www.heritage.org/research /reports/2012/09/marriage-americas-greatest-weapon-against-child -poverty.

6. http://www.wbez.org/series/front-center/parenting-poverty-part-ii -sarahs-story-103474.

7. The New Federal Wedding Tax: How Obamacare Would Dramatically Penalize Marriage, by Robert Rector. January 20, 2010. http://www .heritage.org/research/reports/2010/01/the-new-federal-wedding-tax -how-obamacare-would-dramatically-penalize-marriage.

8. Julia's mother: Why a single mom is better off with a $29,000 job and welfare than taking a $69,000 job, by James Pethokoukis. July 12, 2012. http://www.aei-ideas.org/2012/07/julias-mother-why-a-single-mom -is-better-off-on-welfare-than-taking-a-69000-a-year-job/.

9. http://www.telegraph.co.uk/health/8740278/Women-more-than -twice-as-likely-to-be-depressed.html.

4: CRETINS OF CAMELOT

1. http://www.vanityfair.com/politics/features/2002/04/joekennedy 200204.

2. http://www.vanityfair.com/politics/features/2002/04/joekennedy 200204.

3. *The Sins of the Father: Joseph P. Kennedy and the Dynasty He Founded*, by Ronald Kessler (Warner Books, 1996).

4. http://www.vanityfair.com/politics/features/2002/04/joekennedy 200204.

5. http://www.dailymail.co.uk/news/article-2416511/Robert-Kennedy
-Jnr-sex-diary-proves-infidelity-really-does-run-Kennedy-genes.html.

6. http://www.newsmax.com/RonaldKessler/Rosemary-Kennedy/2008
/06/17/id/324146.

7. http://www.people.com/people/archive/article/0,,20115192,00.html.

8. All the President's Women, by Sara Stewart. November 10, 2013.
http://nypost.com/2013/11/10/all-the-presidents-women-3/.

9. http://www.forbes.com/sites/realspin/2013/10/16/john-f-kennedys
-final-days-reveal-a-man-who-craved-excitement/.

10. http://nypost.com/2013/11/10/all-the-presidents-women-3/.

11. All the President's Women, by Sara Stewart. November 10, 2013.
http://nypost.com/2013/11/10/all-the-presidents-women-3/.

12. http://www.dailymail.co.uk/news/article-2497991/Letters-White
-House-interns-JFK-allegedly-affairs-with.html; http://ricochet.com
/main-feed/What-s-the-Most-Shocking-Part-of-Mimi-Alford-s
-Story.

13. All the President's Women, by Sara Stewart. November 10, 2013.
http://nypost.com/2013/11/10/all-the-presidents-women-3/.

14. http://www.dailymail.co.uk/news/article-2497991/Letters-White
-House-interns-JFK-allegedly-affairs-with.html.

15. It Happened at the Hôtel du Cap, by Cari Beauchamp. March 2009.
http://www.vanityfair.com/style/features/2009/03/dietrich-kennedy
200903.

16. The Unsolved Murder of JFK's Mistress, by Donald E. Wilkes, Jr. May
30, 2012. www.law.uga.edu/dwilkes_more/other_8unsolved_pdf.

17. http://www.forbes.com/sites/realspin/2013/10/16/john-f-kennedys
-final-days-reveal-a-man-who-craved-excitement/.

18. http://www.dailymail.co.uk/news/article-1198991/REVEALED-The
-FBIs-secret-Kennedy-files-showed-Bobby-Jackie-lovers.html.

19. http://nypost.com/2009/07/06/jackies-doomed-love-with-rfk/.

20. http://www.washingtonian.com/bookreviews/biographyhistory
/bobby-and-jackie-a-love-story.php.

21. http://www.people.com/people/archive/article/0,,20115192,00.html.

22. http://www.dailymail.co.uk/debate/article-1209313/Ted-Kennedy
-The-Senator-Sleaze-drunk-sexual-bully—left-young-woman-die.html.

23. http://www.gq.com/news-politics/newsmakers/200704/kennedy-ted
-senator-profile?currentPage=2.

24. http://www.gq.com/news-politics/newsmakers/200704/kennedy-ted
-senator-profile?printable=true.

25. http://www.gq.com/news-politics/newsmakers/200704/kennedy-ted
-senator-profile?currentPage=4.

26. http://www.gq.com/news-politics/newsmakers/200704/kennedy-ted
-senator-profile?printable=true.

27. Kennedy's Darkest Moments, by Michael Scherer. Aug. 27, 2009.
http://content.time.com/time/politics/article/0,8599,1919041,00
.html#ixzz2lgyhqTIA.

28. Kennedy's Darkest Moments, by Michael Scherer. Aug. 27, 2009.
http://content.time.com/time/politics/article/0,8599,1919041,00
.html#ixzz2lgyhqTIA.

29. http://www.people.com/people/archive/article/0,,20115192,00.html.

30. http://www.dailymail.co.uk/news/article-2416511/Robert-Kennedy
-Jnr-sex-diary-proves-infidelity-really-does-run-Kennedy-genes.html.

31. http://www.dailymail.co.uk/news/article-2416511/Robert-Kennedy
-Jnr-sex-diary-proves-infidelity-really-does-run-Kennedy-genes.html.

32. http://www.dailymail.co.uk/news/article-2416511/Robert-Kennedy
-Jnr-sex-diary-proves-infidelity-really-does-run-Kennedy-genes.html.

33. http://www.vanityfair.com/magazine/archive/1992/03/dunne199203.

34. http://www.vanityfair.com/magazine/archive/1992/03/dunne199203.

35. http://www.thesmokinggun.com/documents/crime/william-kennedy
-smith-sleazeball.

36. http://www.nytimes.com/2013/10/24/nyregion/skakel-gets-new-trial
-in-75-killing-of-teenager-in-connecticut.html.

37. http://www.nytimes.com/1997/07/10/us/a-kennedy-faces-the-fallout
-from-a-scandal.html.

38. http://www.eonline.com/news/53169/governator-terminates-groping
-suit.

5: BILL CLINTON, FATHER OF THE YEAR

1. Can Clinton Get the Venus Vote? Women Worry He's From Mars,
by Nina Burleigh. May, 21, 1995. http://www.ninaburleigh.com
/essays/can-clinton-get-the-venus-vote-women-worry-hes-from
-mars.html.

2. http://www.mrc.org/biasalerts/cyberalert-07161998-clinton-shouldnt
-talk#3.

3. http://www.huffingtonpost.com/nina-burleigh/watching-the-clintons-for_b_74965.html.

4. http://www.nytimes.com/1998/03/17/us/testing-president-reaction-willey-interview-shakes-clinton-s-support-among-women.html.

6: THE CLINTON DEMOCREEPS

1. http://www.citynews.ca/2008/03/14/asian-protestors-stage-city-hall-sit-in-over-rob-fords-oriental-comments/.

2. http://www.cbc.ca/news/canada/toronto/ford-admits-lying-to-media-about-drunken-outburst-1.618015.

3. http://www.thestar.com/news/gta/2013/03/08/rob_ford_sarah_thomson_accuses_toronto_mayor_of_inappropriate_touch_suggestive_remark.html.

4. Rob Ford court documents reveal staffers thought prostitute was in his office, mayor was driving drunk, by Sarah Boesveld, Adrian Humphreys, Jake Edmiston, and Peter Kuitenbrouwer. November 13, 2013. http://news.nationalpost.com/2013/11/13/rob-ford-court-documents-reveal-staffers-thought-prostitute-was-in-his-office-mayor-was-driving-drunk/

5. http://www.torontosun.com/2013/11/01/very-intoxicated-rob-ford-was-at-his-worst-st-patricks-day-2012.

6. http://www.sunnewsnetwork.ca/sunnews/politics/archives/2013/11/20131114-072321.html.

7. http://www.torontosun.com/2013/11/07/i-need-f---in-10-minutes-to-make-sure-hes-dead-new-rob-ford-video-surfaces.

8. Nancy Pelosi, Creep-Enabler, by Michelle Malkin. July 24, 2013. http://michellemalkin.com/2013/07/24/nancy-pelosi-creep-enabler/.

9. Mayor Filner Refuses to Address Whirlwind of Allegations, by R. Stickney, Wendy Fry, Gene Cubbison, and Paul Krueger. July 11, 2013. http://www.nbcsandiego.com/news/politics/Donna-Frye-Bob-Filner-Resign-Letter-San-Diego-Mayor--214989091.html.

10. http://www.huffingtonpost.com/2012/03/02/nancy-pelosi-rush-limbaugh-slut-_n_1316472.html.

11. Opinion: San Diego media failed to investigate Filner sooner, by Doug Curlee. July 29, 2013, updated August 22, 2013. http://scoopsandiego.com/columnists/doug_curlee/opinion-san-diego-media

-failed-to-investigate-filner-sooner/article_6fca57f0-f87d-11e2-982e
-001a4bcf6878.html.

12. Carries Fisher's Top 3 Crazy Tales: Senators, Prostitutes and Michael
Jackson, by Sheila Marikar. November 10, 2011. http://abcnews
.go.com/Entertainment/carrie-fishers-top-crazy-tales-senators-prosti
tutes-michael/story?id=14915803#.TrxiDvKwW_8.

13. http://wfpl.org/post/kentucky-statehouse-staffers-accuse-rep-john
-arnold-sexual-harassment-assault.

7: HOW HILLARY CLINTON BROKE THE WOMEN'S MOVEMENT

1. http://emilyslist.org/blog/hillary-clintons-best-moments-secretary
-state.

2. http://www.nydailynews.com/news/politics/u-s-ambassador-accused
-meeting-hookers-public-park-outed-howard-gutman-report-article
-1.1369202.

3. Whistleblower accuses consul general of trysts with subordinates
and hookers, by Kate Briquelet. June 16, 2013. http://nypost
.com/2013/06/16/whistleblower-accuses-consul-general-of-trysts
-with-subordinates-and-hookers/?_ga=1.225479640.37007220.13822
92048.

4. http://nypost.com/2013/06/16/whistleblower-accuses-consul-general
-of-trysts-with-subordinates-and-hookers/?_ga=1.225479640.370072
20.1382292048.

5. http://thecable.foreignpolicy.com/posts/2013/06/17/exclusive
_whistleblower_says_state_department_trying_to_bully_her_into
_silence?wp_login_redirect=0&wp_id_n=2020475913.

6. Exclusive: Whistleblower Says State Department Trying to Bully Her
Into Silence, by John Hudson. June 17, 2013. http://thecable.foreign
policy.com/posts/2013/06/17/exclusive_whistleblower_says_state
_department_trying_to_bully_her_into_silence.

7. On their website is the following mantra: FORCED MOTHER-
HOOD IS FEMALE ENSLAVEMENT. FETUSES ARE NOT
BABIES. ABORTION IS NOT MURDER. WOMEN ARE NOT
INCUBATORS. ABORTION ON DEMAND AND WITHOUT
APOLOGY!

8. Bro-Choice: How #HB2 Hurts Texas Men Who Like Women,

by Ben Sherman. July 3, 2013. http://www.burntorangereport.com /diary/13734/brochoice-how-hb2-hurts-texas-men-who-like-women.

8: BARACK OBAMA: THE MOST ANTI-WOMAN PRESIDENT EVER

1. http://articles.washingtonpost.com/2011-09-16/politics/35274392_1 _ron-suskind-obama-white-house-anita-dunn.
2. Obama Almost Never Golfs With Women, by Keith Koffler. December 6, 2012. http://www.whitehousedossier.com/2012/12/06/obama -golfs-women/.
3. http://www.nytimes.com/2009/10/25/us/politics/25vibe.html?_r=2.
4. http://swampland.time.com/2011/09/21/the-white-house-boys-club -president-obama-has-a-woman-problem/.
5. http://www.csmonitor.com/USA/Politics/The-Vote/2009/1025 /obama-gets-grief-for-male-only-basketball-games.
6. www.breitbart.com/Big-Government/2013/05/10/True-the-vote-IRS.
7. Slow jobs growth for women voters could cost Obama in election. http://thehill.com/blogs/on-the-money/economy/217989-slower-jobs -growth-for-women-voters-could-cost-obama-in-election.
8. http://www.heritage.org/research/reports/2012/09/marriage-americas -greatest-weapon-against-child-poverty.
9. Double Down: Obamacare Will Increase Avg. Individual-Market Insurance Premiums By 99% For Men, 62% For Women, by Avik Roy. September 25, 2013. http://www.forbes.com/sites/theapothecary /2013/09/25/double-down-obamacare-will-increase-avg-individual -market-insurance-premiums-by-99-for-men-62-for-women/.
10. You Also Can't Keep Your Doctor, by Edie Littlefield Sundby. November 3, 2013. http://online.wsj.com/news/articles/SB100014240527023 04527504579171710423780446.
11. Women "Young Invincibles" Not Immune to Premium Rate Increases, by Sam Cappellanti. October 22, 2013. http://americanactionforum .org/research/womenyoung-invincibles-not-immune-to-premium -rate-increases.
12. The "Epidemic" of Sexual Harassment—and Rape—in Morsi's Egypt, by Raymond Ibrahim. February 15, 2013. http://www.frontpagemag .com/2013/raymond-ibrahim/the-epidemic-of-sexual-harassment -and-rape-in-egypt/.

9: THE ABORTION LIE

1. The Hidden Costs, by Tricia Heflin. February 15, 2013. http://ireport .cnn.com/docs/DOC-927821.

2. The Hidden Costs, by Tricia Heflin. February 15, 2013. http://ireport .cnn.com/docs/DOC-927821.

3. Because Abortion Effects Everything!, by Stacy Massey. February 15, 2013. http://ireport.cnn.com/docs/DOC-928192.

4. http://www.rtl.org/prolife_issues/fetaldev_realityofabortion.html.

5. Casual sex can cause depression and even lead to suicidal thoughts, experts warn, by Anna Hodgekiss. November 20, 2013. Updated Nov 21. http://www.dailymail.co.uk/health/article-2510656/Casual-sex-cause -depression-lead-suicidal-thoughts-experts-warn.html.

6. Casual sex can cause depression and even lead to suicidal thoughts, experts warn, by Anna Hodgekiss. November 20, 2013. http://www .dailymail.co.uk/health/article-2510656/Casual-sex-cause-depression -lead-suicidal-thoughts-experts-warn.html.

7. Global study dispels common myths about sex, by Associated Press. October 31, 2006. http://www.nbcnews.com/id/15501173/#.UpwVII 3gJn0.

8. Kermit Gosnell Lived in "Squalor," Had Fleas in Home: CSI, by Vince Lattanzio and David Chang. May 16, 2013. http://www .nbcphiladelphia.com/news/local/Babies-in-Fridge-Feet-in-Cabinets -Found-in-House-of-Horrors-207636681.html.

9. Delaware abortion clinic facing charges of unsafe and unsanitary conditions, by Wendy Saltzman. April 9, 2013. http://abclocal.go.com /wpvi/story?section=news/local&id=9059172.

10. Are There Missing Girls in the United States? Evidence from Birth Data, by Jason Abrevaya. *American Economic Journal: Applied Economics*, 1(2) (2009) 1–34. http://www.aeaweb.org/articles.php?doi=10.1257 /app.1.2.1.

10: HOLLYWOOD HATES WOMEN

1. Seeing You Seeing Me: The Trouble With 'Blue Is the Warmest Color,' by Manohla Dargis. October 25, 2013. http://www.ny times.com/2013/10/27/movies/the-trouble-with-blue-is-the-warmest -color.html?pagewanted=1&_r=0.

2. Women Can't Gain Influence in Hollywood Because Women Don't

Look like Men, by Liz Garcia. August 24, 2012. http://www.forbes.com/sites/lizgarcia/2012/08/24/women-cant-gain-influence-in-hollywood-because-women-dont-look-like-men/.

3. Swedish cinemas take aim at gender bias with Bechdel test rating, by Associated Press in Stockholm. November 6, 2013. http://www.theguardian.com/world/2013/nov/06/swedish-cinemas-bechdel-test-films-gender-bias.

4. How Hollywood made its heroines weight-obsessed and man mad, by Amelia Hill. February 7, 2009. http://www.theguardian.com/film/2009/feb/08/hollywood-cinema-female-leads.

5. It's a Man's (Celluloid) World: On-Screen Representations of Female Characters in the Top 100 Films of 2011, by Martha M. Lauzen, Ph.D. 2012. http://www.wif.org/images/repository/pdf/other/2011-its-a-mans-world-exec-summ.pdf.

6. Screening Sexy: Film Females and the Story That Isn't Changing. May 13, 2013. http://annenberg.usc.edu/News%20and%20Events/News/130513SmithStudy.aspx.

7. Hollywood's Challenge: Where Are the Women Directors? http://www.fandor.com/infographics/where-are-the-women-directors.

8. How One Group of Producers is Looking to Solve Hollywood's Female Problem, by Dan Solomon. 2013. http://www.fastcocreate.com/3019780/how-one-group-of-producers-is-looking-to-solve-hollywoods-female-problem.

9. Why the Odds Are Still Stacked Against Women in Hollywood, by Kim Masters. December 9, 2011. http://www.hollywoodreporter.com/news/angelina-jolie-kristen-stewart-emma-watson-katheryn-bigelow-269694.

10. Why the Odds Are Still Stacked Against Women in Hollywood, by Kim Masters. December 9, 2011. http://www.hollywoodreporter.com/news/angelina-jolie-kristen-stewart-emma-watson-katheryn-bigelow-269694.

11. Why the Odds Are Still Stacked Against Women in Hollywood, by Kim Masters. December 9, 2011. http://www.hollywoodreporter.com/news/angelina-jolie-kristen-stewart-emma-watson-katheryn-bigelow-269694.

12. Melissa Joan Hart: 'These Days I Find More Republicans in Hollywood,' by Cavan Sieczkowski. November 5, 2013. http://www

.huffingtonpost.com/2013/11/05/melissa-joan-hart-republicans
-hollywood_n_4218426.html.

11: THE NRA: AMERICA'S REAL PRO-WOMEN'S GROUP

1. davekopel.org/Testimony-Senate-Judiciary-Kopel-1-30-13.pdf.
2. http://news.google.com/newspapers?nid=1129&dat=19910406&id=v
   -FRAAAAIBAJ&sjid=bm4DAAAAIBAJ&pg=4660,1780493.
3. http://kdvr.com/2013/02/18/conservatives-take-aim-at-democrat-for
   -statement-about-rape/.
4. http://www.gwhatchet.com/2010/08/26/sex-offenders-live-work-in
   -foggy-bottom/.
5. http://www.crimelibrary.com/notorious_murders/classics/brianna
   _denison/2.html.
6. NRA News Interview.

ACKNOWLEDGMENTS

Since the focus of this book is on female independence, empowerment, and strength, I'll start by thanking the people who helped me build mine. My family is full of unyielding women who have influenced me and I'm sure proud of it. Thanks to my mother, whose incredible capabilities in all areas of life never cease to amaze me. *Assault and Flattery* wouldn't have happened without her. For my late great-aunt Meri Pavlich Roby, whose impeccable leadership skills and class allowed her to trailblaze through the women's movement, leaving a path, and a legacy, for me to follow.

To my brother, thanks for letting me boss you around when we were young. I think it paid off. To my dad, thanks always for your faith in me and never-ending encouragement. Buz and Sonja Mills, your support has meant more than you know.

Thank you to all the wonderful people at Simon & Schuster. Thanks especially to my editors Mitchell Ivers and Natasha Simons and production editor Al Madocs for their diligence and patience. A special thanks to Threshold president Louise Burke for her enthusiasm and to art director Lisa Litwack and photographer Claudio Marinisco for their creative vision. Thanks to attorney John Pelosi for making sure I wasn't too hard on the Kennedys.

Thanks as well to the team at Javelin. Keith Urbahn and Matt Latimer believed in me from the beginning and we've come a long way since they started their company a few short years ago in Washington, D.C.

A sincere and humble thanks to Jonathan Garthwaite, my boss at Townhall. Without his confidence and faith in my ability to succeed and take risks, projects like this wouldn't happen. The flexibility he has given me to pursue special projects since I started in Washington four years ago is invaluable. My gratitude is also extended to the entire Townhall team for their support and help, especially to Guy Benson and Dan Doherty. During the course of writing this book, I asked Dan to help me out and cover for me countless times. Although it added to his daily workload, he never said no.

My thanks go to Michelle Malkin, a woman who not only inspires me every day but has been gracious enough with her time to listen to my ideas. Thanks to Dana Perino, who has opened up a number of doors to opportunity for me and has selflessly offered her mentorship and advice. The same goes for Sean Hannity, who has gone out of his way to help me take my skills and ideas to another level. I am grateful to Monica Crowley not only for her generous support, but for her infectious, never-ending girl-power attitude. Thanks to David Limbaugh for all his support of my first book, giving me the confidence to write the second one.

Thanks to all the people who took the time to do interviews for this book, especially Amanda Collins, Governor Mitt Romney, and Christy McCormick.

For my friends and family, thank you as always for your patience, understanding, and encouragement throughout the book-writing process. Special thanks to Erika Johnsen—she has been an incredible, insightful, and encouraging friend.

Last, my thanks to the National Organization for Women and other feminists, whose endless capacity for nonsense made this book a joy to write.

To anyone I have forgotten, please know you are greatly appreciated.

INDEX